Foundational Flows

Using Jin Shin Jyutsu and the Astrological Birth Chart
to Create Flow between Soul and Spirit

Awakening and Facilitating the Alchemical Wedding
of Soul and Spirit

The Foundational Level Course

Stan Posey L. Ac.

Copyright © 2020 Stan Posey

All rights reserved. No part of this publication may be reproduced, distributed, or transmitted in any form or by any means, including photocopying, recording, or other electronic or mechanical methods, without the prior written permission of the publisher, except in the case of brief quotations embodied in critical reviews and certain other noncommercial uses permitted by copyright law. For permission requests, write to books@erbdoc.com.

Stan Posey
3208 E. Fort Lowell Road, Suite 103
Tucson, AZ 85716
erbdoc.com

Ordering Information:
For details, contact books@erbdoc.com.

Production by
Mesquite Media
mesquite-media.com

Printed in the United States of America.

First Edition

Contents

Preface iii
Acknowledgements iv
Order your own v
    Personalized Foundational Flows v
        Self-Help Finger Sequences based on your Foundational Flows v
Foreword vi
Introduction vii
    Introducing the players vii
Chapter 1 1
    Jin Shin Jyutsu (JSJ) introduction 1
Chapter 2 4
    Astrology introduction and common ways of combining with JSJ 4
Chapter 3 12
    Thinking, Feeling and Willing - The Foundational Keys 12
Chapter 4 18
    Zodiacal differentiations and associations 18
Chapter 5 22
    Harmonizing soul and spirit with flow 22
Chapter 6 29
    Finding the Organ Flow patterns to be used as derived from the natal chart . 29
Chapter 7 31
    How to use the Foundational Flows 31
Chapter 8 34

A word about the sessions – timing and frequency 34

Chapter 9 35
The Fly in the Ointment - Astral vs Etheric Body 35

Chapter 10 45
More on Thinking, Feeling and Willing at this Foundational Level 45

Chapter 11 50
Rudolf Steiner and Christian Rosenkreutz 50

Chapter 12 53
Depths with Fingers – 53

Chapter 13 58
Bringing in 'Self-Help' based on the Foundational Flows Individualized Finger Sequences and Mudras 58

Chapter 14 67
Other relationship qualities of exploration 67
    Sayings for the signs - Organ qualities - Numbers 67
    Flow - Essence/Project/Virtues 67

Chapter 15 77
Foundational Flow Mudras and the Foundation Stone Meditation 77

Chapter 16 86
Closing the Foundation – Looking ahead 86

Appendix 1 88
Some paths emerging from the heart of Ageless Wisdom 88
    The 'Six Accessory Exercises' – Rudolf Steiner 89
    The 'Eightfold Path' and Rudolf Steiner 90
    Initiation prior to the Mystery of Golgotha - Rudolf Steiner 93

    The Rosicrucian Method – 7 Steps 94

    7 steps - Esoteric Christianity – Rudolf Steiner 95

    Petalamund (Petal Mount) 96

Appendix 2 .... **99**

  Eurythmy 99

Appendix 3 .... **100**

  A brief list of the numbered meanings 1 – 26 Safety Energy Locks 100

About the Author **103**

"There is a knighthood of our time whose members do not ride
Through the darkness of physical forests as of old,
But through the forests of darkened minds;
They are armored with a spiritual armor
And an inner sun makes them radiant;
Out of them shines healing—
Healing that flows from the knowledge of the image of mankind as spiritual being.
They must create inner order, inner justice, peace, and conviction
In the darkness of our time.
They must know that they walk with angels."

Karl Konig

Preface

To reap the powerful personalized health benefits of centering and stress reduction found in this book you don't have to be a Jin Shin Jyutsu (JSJ) practitioner or an astrologer. You don't have to be into Anthroposophy or Esoteric Christianity. You don't have to be on the path of Rosicrucian alchemy, yoga or any 'spiritual path' at all. This book is about finding quick and easy access to that personalized silent point of power within all of us which is the place where all of these paths meet.

All of these paths are rooted in 'Ageless Wisdom', also called 'Primeval Wisdom'. Interconnections between many of these arts will be pointed out for the benefit of anyone interested.

The purpose of this text is to explain the underlying rational of how these arts are combined in a way that is personalized to you, the individual. This is so that you can have a powerful tool to assist you in going through this life with the 'projects' YOU came in to work on and evolve. You don't need to know all this to work with this tool. You can use it for stress relief and leave it at that. But you can also benefit from opening your awareness to the underlying unity found in the Ageless Wisdom as found at the foundation and center of all the above mentioned paths.

As a Jin Shin Jyutsu practitioner you can help your clients by finding their Foundational Flows and working together using them. A way will also be shown of using this tool that is accessed within the wisdom of Jin Shin Jyutsu Self-Help. This allows any individual to be able to use this tool on their own.

Acknowledgements

I first have to thank my Angel and all the various ancestors and spiritual mentors, family and friends, both seen and unseen, that have helped keep me on task.

Of course from the beginning I always wanted to know it all now. But, thankfully, the driving mantra of my life has been the Taurus ideal that 'Perseverance furthers' and so onward I go…

I especially have to thank my wife, Sara Harper - first for introducing me to Jin Shin Jyutsu and second for the encouragement in developing and executing these Foundational Flows in practice. As you will see the Foundational Flows are optimally done in 'triads', the two of us would do these 'two-sided' flows on a 'receiver.' I could have never followed through in the full development of these ideas without her patient and enthusiastic participation. This goes as well for those people who volunteered to receive these Foundational Flows in the beginning phases of this development and all the ones who have followed.

I would also like to thank my father, Clay Posey, who was a renowned equine veterinarian. He taught, by example, the value of being open to "whatever works," in the sense of exploring even "unorthodox" modalities.

There have been many practitioners who get the Foundational Flows to work with their clients. And many more who get the Self-Help finger sequences for their clients to do for themselves.

Without these willing souls I could never have had the encouraging feedback to follow this project through.

Order your own
Personalized Foundational Flows

Or

Self-Help Finger Sequences based on your Foundational Flows

Order online at https://erbdoc.com/flows or complete and mail this form to:

Stan Posey, 3208 E. Fort Lowell Rd., Suite 103, Tucson, AZ 85716

Please send based on my information below:

❑ Personalized Foundational Flows - $25

❑ Self-Help Finger Sequences based on my Foundational Flows - $25

❑ Both Personalized Foundational Flows & Self-Help Finger Sequences - $45

Full name: _____

Date of birth: _____

Time of birth (if known; should be on Birth Certificate): _____

Place of birth: _____

Email address to send information to: _____

Payment (Visa/MasterCard/Discover/American Express):

Credit card number: _____ - _____ - _____ - _____

Expiration date (MM/YY): _____ CSV code: _____

Name on card: _____

Foreword

"...as we live our days on earth, we discover aspects of ourselves in meeting the invitations to our becoming offered by the others in our lives. Our "I"......lives in the people and circumstances we meet, it waits to be incorporated, to be taken up by us, to be developed in ever new ways."

~Signe Eklund Schaefer ~ as quoted in Foundational Flows.

In an extraordinary exploration of the Alchemical Wedding – the marriage of soul and spirit - Stan Posey offers a crucible: Foundational Flows. If your heart, too, desires your own "becoming", may Stan be one of the people you meet, may Foundational Flows be one of the circumstances.

Foundational Flows is a walkabout in which a young man's disenchantment with a too narrow "scientific" view, becomes, over time and through unending curiosity, deep study and faith, a restoration of "the heart of the art" of healing.

Stan invites us to join him – not in a 'text book', though there is much to learn – but in a conversation. A transmission. A most comprehensive collection of possibilities both humble and stunning, carefully rewoven from the ancient threads of Jin Shin Jyutsu, Astrology, Acupuncture, Anthroposophy, and other wise and trusted traditions. Delivered to us "ever new".

May you take up Stan's invitation, discover in Foundational Flows the chapters, the experiences, the treasures, that belong to you. May your 'projects' find new ground beneath them. May you find the practitioners who can support you and the clients who are ripe for the enlivening. May you know yourself Whole. Home. Strong. Blessed. May you find wonder in the living body, the deep soul and the strong spirit that is you.

Offered in grateful appreciation for the *experience* of Foundational Flows offered by Stan Posey and Sara Harper, one on my left side and one on my right, blessed, holy presence....

Linda Kerr

Introduction
Introducing the players

Jin Shin Jyutsu (JSJ), Astrology and the harmonizing of soul and spirit

As a younger man, in acupuncture school many years ago, I became very frustrated with the education. I had already taken many years of western sciences at the university level and found that this ancient medical art was being taught in a very modern, non-traditional way. I knew that it can be difficult for a western culturally conditioned mind to grasp the more subtle aspects of eastern wisdom teachings. But it seemed to me that the art was being castrated in favor of the science. I understood that it was being westernized in an attempt to make it 'scientifically valid'.

But what I saw was the same as what I had just come out of in the university, with increasingly less and less of the art. What I experienced was the same labeling process that happens in 'generalization', when it is emphasized at the cost of the individual.

What I mean is that we were being taught that 'this box' of symptoms is treated by 'this box' of points or herbs. A heavy emphasis was on the labeling that takes place by using the names of syndromes and diseases. It leaves one blind-sided by the fact that in reality there is never just one of these labels occurring, it is always a melting pot of factors creating this individual person's imbalance.

We figure this out through experience in practice, but generalized labeling is a dangerous judgment that the western mind likes to impose onto individuals. Yes, it can help us navigate through a complicated world, but it also keeps us from being able to differentiate between the forest and the trees.

This is fine as far as it goes but not at the cost of losing the heart of the art. And the heart of the art, as I saw it, was the beauty found in seeing the wholeness of an individual – body, soul and spirit. The ancient oriental healing arts have retained this recognition within their very structure and cosmology. It is this same aspect which western medicine had mostly lost by its heavy emphasis on the scientific method which by its very structure can only measure quantities and not qualities. The good news is that we are seeing an explosion of integration that will eventually bring wholeness back to medicine, as well as to society, which will someday be the norm.

But at that time of my life I found it extremely frustrating and sought for ways to remedy this. I was always voraciously curious and had been exploring different esoteric traditions for some time. It was when I was 29 that I said out loud 'why is my life so hard' when a voice in my head said very clearly "Saturn, teacher, taskmaker, 29 years". At this point I told myself that I would find out if Saturn's cycle was 29 years, and if it was then I was going to study astrology. And so I soon discovered the single best self-learning tool that I have ever come across.

This might not make sense to everyone but it helped me with finding and understanding the heart and the art of Chinese medicine. Eastern arts have many archetypal ideas and pictures which are always alive, moving and changing form. For example, the 5 Elements, also called the 5 Phases, as well as ideas like yin and yang. These are different ways of dividing the world up into 2 qualitative gestures or 5 qualitative gestures.

But they are not static labels; they are living archetypes upon which emphasis is on the living and ever changing relationships between the archetypes, instead of on the archetypes as objects, like in the west.

This is a huge difference between the eastern and western worldviews. Astrological traditions also come from ancient sources and are heavy in archetypal pictures. When so understood it can become very alive. Studying these archetypes helped me more deeply understand the archetypes in Chinese medicine.

I was already studying the work of Rudolf Steiner since my early 20's. Serendipity also drove me deeper into the study of his works. Through all of my early and various studies I would eventually circle back to his work and it was always deeply resonant within my heart. It was Steiner's cosmology that could hold the

Foundational Flows

fullness of all that I was learning and to this day it holds my understanding together in a beautiful vibrantly alive form.

The next piece of the puzzle, which makes up the bulk of the work presented here, comes from Jin Shin Jyutsu. In Jin Shin Jyutsu I found another cosmology that fit into the rest of my work. What Jin Shin Jyutsu added was the uniqueness of bringing the macrocosm down into the microcosm as a harmonizing influence through the use of our own hands. Here we get to share in the work of the creator in easing discomfort and dis-ease. The only requirement is to keep the ego out of the way, put your hands on someone, and just be a jumper cable of the creator's infinite blessing. The extra beauty is that by understanding the cosmology we can use it in ever deepening ways specific to the individual. I was sold.

Usually in the Jin Shin Jyutsu classes I've taken I have often said (only half-jokingly), that if I had it all to do over, I would 'just' be a Jin Shin Jyutsu practitioner. This is because we have our tools everywhere we go, our hands. But I also often say that when I grow up I want to be a travelling astrosopher priest. So really I have to give thanks for my journey and to who I am because of my eclectic nature. And it is in finding the core essence of, and synthesizing these various arts and views into a holistic mechanism, that this work can come about.

Chapter 1
Jin Shin Jyutsu (JSJ) introduction

Jin Shin Jyutsu is a Japanese hands-on art of relaxing and balancing the body, soul and spirit. Jin Shin Jyutsu is an art that addresses this 3-fold nature of our being as that represents the 3 worlds which we simultaneously inhabit. These 3 worlds are addressed by the 3 aspects of Jin Shin Jyutsu known as Physio-Philosophy, Physio-Psychology and Physio-Physiology. As a hands-on art it connects these 3 worlds through the simplicity of putting the hands on what are known as Safety Energy Locks (SEL's or, in the original Japanese, Eki Ten – 'Divine Fluid Being') and being a 'jumper cable' to facilitate flow.

Jin Shin Jyutsu is described as an innate awareness. If we are observant we notice that all of us naturally use Jin Shin Jyutsu without even noticing it. People have natural ways that they hold themselves in particular situations. The clues to the meaning behind this are held within the wisdom of the SEL's. The beauty of the art is enhanced by the 'organ flow patterns' which have been devised to enhance or open the flow of qi (life force energy) when it is blocked or inhibited.

One can seek out a practitioner of the art for sessions and one can learn the extraordinary gift of Self-Help that one can use oneself.

The art was rediscovered in Japan by Jiro Murai. He healed himself by using the art and then dedicated himself to it. He was allowed access to the Imperial archive after healing a member of the royal family. It was here that he discovered the arts foundational roots in what is known as Ageless Wisdom. This is the wisdom which goes back to our divine roots before recorded history. Jin Shin Jyutsu is rooted in the same source as Acupuncture of which we find such similarity.

The world was blessed the day Jiro Murai asked Mary Iino (who became Mary Burmeister) to bring the gift of this art to America. Mary studied and combined this art of Ageless Wisdom with the esoteric traditions of the west to make it more palatable to the understanding of the western mind. But the depth of this wisdom keeps it beyond any complete understanding by the intellect and this helps it maintain its hold on the divine mystery behind its source. It is this mystery of the creator, as the living source, which we can simply let go and connect with by being 'jumper cables'.

The beauty of the cosmology behind this art helped me fill in some of the questions I had about some of the deeper aspects of Chinese medicine. This opened up doors and hallways to a new reverential admiration of both arts. It is my hope that the work I will show of combining Jin Shin Jyutsu with astrology for the harmonizing of soul and spirit will prove beneficial for the reader and those who choose to practice these arts in this way.

Besides the Jin Shin Jyutsu textbooks and Self-Help texts by Mary Burmeister, there is a wonderful book, "The Touch of Healing" by Alice Burmeister and Tom Monte. If you are not familiar with Jin Shin Jyutsu I would highly recommend starting with this book if you would like to know more. It gives a background to all the Safety Energy Locks, the Depths and Attitudes, as well as quickies to harmonize the organ flow patterns. It is a great resource for using the fingers in Self Help and introduces the traditional finger mudras. It is also a great resource to learn more about the history of this art.

Just as a crossover to help those interested in Acupuncture and Chinese medicine, the Jin Shin Jyutsu 'Depths' correspond with what we call the 5 Elements, or 5 Phases (the more living description). There are only 26 SEL's but I have a book in process showing the deeper relationships with acupuncture.

The 3 worlds that I have hinted at (a universal trinity which shows up everywhere) can also be seen in what Jin Shin Jyutsu calls Bustline, Waistline and Hipline. These correspond with the 3 burners or Jiao's in Chinese Medicine. These are also reflective of the organs within each burner as well as the 3 main divisions in the positions of the pulse.

Jin Shin Jyutsu also gives us the Main Central Vertical Universal Harmonizing Energy, the Major Vertical Supervisor Universal Harmonizing Energy and the Diagonal Mediator Universal Harmonizing Energy as an even more primordial level of connection to the 3 worlds reflected in our 3-fold nature. These 3 are the fundamental core "Trinity flows" of Jin Shin Jyutsu. They are related to the manifesting blueprint of our Being.

Having listed these resources I don't feel that we need to go specifically into organ flow patterns and the numbered flows from Jin Shin Jyutsu in this book. All of the flow patterns are found in Text 1 and 2 by Mary Burmeister. I will here only refer to finding the individualized Foundational Flows as based upon the natal chart and how to use them with our idea of the synching of flow between soul and spirit. In taking a class based on this book we will go more deeply into the flows as well as experience them in our bodies with hands-on sessions.

Chapter 2
Astrology introduction and common ways of combining with JSJ

Our astrological birth chart is a snapshot of the 'projects' we have chosen, with divine guidance, to work on in the current lifetime. These 'projects' reflect the karma that has ripened to work on in this incarnation. These projects show us the inherent bias through which we experience our world. These 'projects' get expressed on an emotional level by our 'attitudes', which is a direct expression of these unconscious karmic biases being played out in daily life. It is through consciously recognizing and harmonizing these 'projects' that we can continually evolve.

There are many ways that we can combine the understanding of Jin Shin Jyutsu with what we can learn from our natal or birth chart. For example, we could always use the Sun, Moon and Ascendant positions at birth to determine which Jin Shin Jyutsu organ flow patterns could be chosen to assist our constitutional level well-being. We can choose these flows because this trinity is the most personal part of each chart for any individual. They are the most personal points because they are the fastest moving points in the chart.

The Ascendant, or Rising sign, is the point showing the eastern horizon at birth. It represents the starting point of the wheel of houses in the horoscope. This wheel moves approximately $1°$ every four minutes, making one complete revolution over the course of one day. The Moon cycle is completed every 29.5 days. The Sun returns every year. They are the 3 most personal parts of the chart because of this speed. The further out we go in the solar system, the planetary cycles become longer and longer, to the point where the outer planets are much more generational in influence than personal.

Foundational Flows

The essential question regarding the overall relationships within the chart then becomes how does your more personalized planetary trinity fit into and work within these more generational and collective influences.

Since the natal chart shows the 'projects' we came in to work on and evolve, it only makes sense that by supporting this planetary trinity, and all that it represents, we can be assisted in accomplishing our intended tasks for this life. The more conscious this work is the more it can evolve.

We must keep in mind that the Ascendant is a point in space and not a planet. Because of its position as the East, or Rising point, it has extra importance. It helps emphasize our particular relationship to the world. The wheel of the horoscope, divided into 12 houses, represents our particular relationship to our inner and outer world. We can see the Ascendant as our own personalized way that we are oriented to this wheel of life.

By knowing the zodiacal signs in which this trinity resides we can use the cosmology of Jin Shin Jyutsu to determine which organ flow patterns are represented which we can then use to assist us in our evolutionary journey. Using the supporting organ flow patterns for the trinity will always be helpful for us since they are so primary and personalized. Because of this they can be thought of as 'astrological trinity flows' for the individual whose natal chart we are looking at.

We can use the following example –

If someone has the Sun in Aquarius at birth we will see that the organ flow pattern associated with Aquarius is Gall Bladder function energy. If the Moon was in Scorpio, the associated organ flow pattern is for Kidney function energy. And if it was Leo Rising at birth, as the Ascendant, then the organ flow pattern of choice is Heart function energy.

We see then that these 3 organ flow patterns will always be supportive in this person's life journey and will always be a good choice for them to use. This will especially hold true during times of stress in a person's life. Stress always affects each one of us differently based upon our own individual constitutional strengths and weaknesses. These Trinity flows show some of our most important personal 'projects' in life and they will represent a 'constitutional need' for support.

Another example of how to use Jin Shin Jyutsu organ flow patterns based upon a natal chart is by bringing in the specific timing and movement of planetary cycles relative to our personal life cycles. Let's say we are having a Mars return, which happens roughly every 2 years, we might choose the organ flow pattern associated with that Mars position to assist ourselves through that planetary cycle. This cycle will be calling us to bring a new energy and awareness to help us evolve with this particular 'project'.

We can use the following example –

If the natal Mars is in Sagittarius we will see that the Jin Shin Jyutsu organ flow pattern associated with Sagittarius is called Diaphragm function energy. (The equivalent organ in traditional Chinese medical terminology is Pericardium). We can see then that the Diaphragm function energy will need extra help throughout this life cycle.

This will hold true for any of the planetary cycles that we live through. One more example might be a return of Venus found in the birth chart in Pisces. We will see that the organ flow pattern associated with Pisces is Liver function energy and so can be chosen to assist this individual through that cycle.

These return cycles are when a planet returns through time to its natal or birth position. I would like to hint at 2 other ways to combine astrology and Jin Shin Jyutsu before we get down to our special topic of the Foundational Flows.

Other ways of looking at certain timing of events in our biography are based upon using what are called 'transits' and 'progressions'. This can involve any planetary combination. Transits and progressions are similar in their effect but are derived differently.

Foundational Flows

A transit is when, on a given day, any planet might be at the same position in the sky as one of our natal planets was at our birth. Now this does not mean that the planet 'out there' is necessarily causing an effect upon us. But there is a synchronistic and symbolic resonance of the timing of this transit with what we experience in our inner and outer life. This may best be explained with the ancient hermetic axiom, "As Above, So Below". There is a similarity in the gesture of the symbolic meaning of the planets, signs and angles (called aspects) of the relationship of the planets involved in these transits. This resonates with the events we experience both inwardly and outwardly in our lives. Carl Jung would use the term synchronicity. Steven Forrest tells us that the ancient Druid priests would call it the 'wyrd', that interconnecting web of meaning that holds everything together.

This is similar to what happens during progressions, which is another way of the timing of events after birth and during our lives. Describing how these are derived is not our purpose here, and there are several types.

What is important is the information provided by the symbols involved in this meeting of planets as meaningful archetypes. From this we can choose the appropriate organ flow patterns to help maintain harmony through what can be experienced as stressful times.

In using transits and progressions to determine helpful Jin Shin Jyutsu organ flow patterns to assist our growth process we will here emphasize what might be called the 'hard' ones. There should never be a judgement of good or bad placements within a birth chart. It is best to see it as representing the 'projects' we are here to work on and refine in ourselves. The times when we are called to become more conscious of our 'projects' to work on them can be stressful experiences.

We can use as a guide, within the above context, that some planetary symbols might represent a more difficult period of time with a transit or progression than another symbol. This is also true of the angular relationship of the symbols involved, the aspects themselves.

This angular relationship is called an 'aspect'. It shows the degree of relationship within the 360° of possibility inside the wheel of the horoscope. Some angles, like some planets, are generally thought of as being more difficult than others. But I must emphasize that this has to be considered within the broader context of the whole chart and the individual involved.

For example –

A Saturn transit or progression to a natal planet is generally considered to have a heavier energy and can be one of the more difficult ones. But let's just point out that part of the gesture of the symbol of Saturn is hard work. And if we flow with the timing of this event and apply hard work toward some goal or project it can pay off in a big way. That can become a positive usage of this energy of tension.

So working with the energy in the appropriate way is what is important. If we do not heed that call then certainly things may seem more difficult.

So what is the best way to use Jin Shin Jyutsu in these circumstances?

The so-called 'harder' aspects of transits and progressions can certainly signify more stressful times in our lives. So one way to choose a Jin Shin Jyutsu organ flow pattern to support us through that stress might be the following -

We will limit ourselves in this example to the 4th harmonic set of aspect relations. This set of relationships includes conjunction (0^0), square (90^0, 270^0) and opposition (180^0). These are considered the 'hard' aspect angles, and can reflect a stressful time no matter which of the planets and symbols are involved in the timing of these events.

Example – Transiting Uranus squaring natal Mercury in Capricorn. We would want to support the Mercury position and its relationships. Uranus transits release a lot of energy and the square aspect makes it a likely time of stress. Uranus moves slowly so the organ flow pattern to support Umbilicus function energy (Triple Burner in TCM) should be done for extra support throughout the duration of this transit. Umbilicus function energy is chosen because it is the organ flow pattern associated with Capricorn. The Mercury is in Capricorn at birth, the Uranus transits it by square aspect, the organ flow pattern to support the Mercury is chosen by the sign the Mercury is in.

The same goes for progressions (these can be Secondary progressions or Solar Arc progressions).

Example – if Solar Arc progressed Mars is squaring natal Moon in Scorpio we would like to do extra Kidney organ flow pattern to support the person through this time cycle. The birth Moon being in Scorpio shows us the organ flow pattern we need to support. For Scorpio this organ flow pattern is for Kidney function energy.

As a side note for Jin Shin Jyutsu practitioners. We would know that this is not the only flow to help with supporting Kidney function energy. Another of many choices would be to use 'Reversing and Increasing the 4th Depth' as an additional flow to support the person through this time period when the Kidney gesture of our nature is being stressed. There would be several choices to support Kidney function energy based upon the practitioner's level of understanding. But the primary organ flow pattern for Scorpio is Kidney function energy.

I would like to hint at one other way in which the natal chart can be used to determine which flows to use to support a person through their 'projects'. This is a method that I learned from long-time Jin Shin Jyutsu instructor Carlos Gutterres. I don't wish to steal his thunder and so will only give the underlying idea. If someone wants to learn the full technique, they can do so through him.

The basic idea is that he lays out the signs in a template form, filling in the template with the planets in their proper positions. This filled in template is then used to determine the Bustline, Waistline and Hipline (another trinity found in JSJ) predominance and emphasis in the chart. From this, organ flow patterns are chosen to help support the 'projects' being emphasized specific to that individual. This is another way to address supporting the individual though their constitutional needs based on the natal or birth chart.

I have found this to be a profound insight and very useful. Thank you, Carlos!

Foundational Flows

We have so far introduced and reviewed some of the various ways that the astrological information contained in a natal chart can help us use Jin Shin Jyutsu to support a person through the trials and tribulations of their personal 'projects'.

However, these are not the techniques that we will be emphasizing in this work. We will be specifically looking to help synchronize flow between soul and spirit as indicated in the birth chart. Although some of the above discussed techniques can be used in conjunction with what we will share regarding this harmonizing of flow, they will only be considered as secondary techniques of support for this larger goal of flow and union between soul and spirit.

But before we move on to that discussion let us take a look at the organ flow pattern associations with the signs as found within Jin Shin Jyutsu cosmology. This gives us the framework for finding the corresponding organ flow patterns to support the various projects emphasized by having planets in any given sign as found in the natal chart.

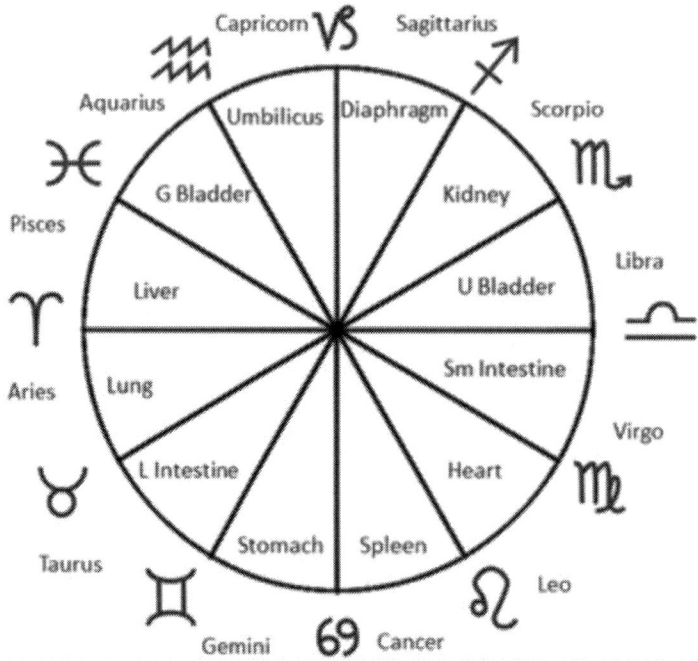

Wheel showing Jin Shin Jyutsu organ flow patterns with associated Zodiacal signs above and table below.

Foundational Flows

Aries	♈	Lung
Taurus	♉	Large Intestine
Gemini	♊	Stomach
Cancer	♋	Spleen
Leo	♌	Heart
Virgo	♍	Small Intestine
Libra	♎	Urinary Bladder
Scorpio	♏	Kidney
Sagittarius	♐	Diaphragm (Heart Protector)
Capricorn	♑	Umbilicus (Triple Burner)
Aquarius	♒	Gall Bladder
Pisces	♓	Liver

Chapter 3
Thinking, Feeling and Willing - The Foundational Keys

Rudolf Steiner talked about the consciousness of our soul having three main qualities – thinking, feeling and willing. Understanding, tracking and developing these 3 qualities are the foundation of the work of the alchemical marriage of soul and spirit. Ultimately, this is what the work presented here is all about, supporting this awakening of the connection to our Higher Self.

In all the old myths and fairy tales the sleeping princess is representing the soul. This sleeping soul is awaiting the awakening kiss of consciousness from the prince, the Higher Self. But for this an individual has to develop the soul forces of thinking, feeling and willing, to build the bridge for this awakening kiss of consciousness.

I will be pointing ultimately to Steiner's work as a modern way that is appropriate for the developing of this deepening. But within this work we will be showing how the natal chart indicates specific ways to start this process of flow and integration using the hands-on techniques of Jin Shin Jyutsu already indicated.

My hope is that, especially for those who are already on their spiritual path, these insights and techniques will further facilitate and enhance their work in that direction. But it should certainly be helpful for anyone's well-being since it is a way of individualizing the techniques available through Jin Shin Jyutsu to enhance flow as it regards their own personal 'projects'. 'Flow' is the perfect word here because it is in our 'projects' that we are stuck in the patterns of consciousness that get expressed as 'attitude'.

In the introduction it was shown that there are several ways of using the birth chart to combine the JSJ organ flow patterns to support our working with the 'projects' we have in this life. Here we will begin to show another way of working with this natal chart to begin the foundational work of harmonizing flow between soul and spirit.

Foundational Flows

It might generally be assumed that, following the general introduction, it is the positions of the Sun, Moon and Ascendant that we are using to build this bridge of flow. But we will now see that this is not the case. What was said in the introduction about this trinity and their associated organ flow patterns as always being supportive is certainly still true. But we will now see that there are other specific levels of connections indicated for this work.

The work being developed here is truly alchemical at its core. It is about developing the bridge of flow between the soul and the Higher Self. True alchemical work has to be consciously attended to and that is why the work presented here is to be seen as an addition to the work one is actively undertaking along their spiritual path.

These individual paths may be numerous, and again I will be pointing to Steiner's work with emphasis, but these Foundational Flows will be helpful for anyone regardless of their path. I will later expand what is meant by the idea of 'alchemy'. But now we will begin to identify the indicators of what we find within the chart that is in need of being alchemically transformed.

"There are three aspects to our human nature ... body, soul and spirit... Through the body, we are capable of linking ourselves for the moment to things outside us. Through the soul, we preserve the impressions things make on us. Through the spirit, what the things themselves contain is disclosed to us. Only when we look at the human being from these three sides can we hope to understand our true nature, for these three sides show us that we are related to the rest of the world in a threefold way...The domain of the soul is inaccessible to bodily perception. Our bodily existence is there for all to see, but we carry our soul existence inside us as our own private world. Through the spirit, however, the outer world is revealed to us in a higher way... Thus as human beings we are citizens of three worlds. In body, we both belong to and perceive the outer world; in soul, we build up our own inner world; and in spirit, a third world that is higher than both of the others reveals itself to us...

Foundational Flows

Feeling follows closely on sensation, with one sensation arousing pleasure in us and another displeasure. These are the stirrings of our inner soul life. We each create an inner world of feelings in addition to the world that works in on us from outside. Then there is (another) factor, our will, through which we work back upon the outside world, leaving the imprint of our own inner being on it. In will activity, the soul flows outward, in a sense. The fact that our actions bear the stamp of our inner life distinguishes them from natural events taking place in the outer world. In this way the soul sets itself up as something personal and private in contrast to the world outside. It receives stimuli from the outer world, but constructs an inner private world in accordance with them. Bodily existence becomes the basis for soul existence…

The soul element in a human being is not determined exclusively by the body. We do not wander aimlessly and without direction from one sense impression to another, nor do we respond to every random stimulus that acts on us from outside or through our bodily processes. Instead, we think about our sensations and our actions. By thinking about our sensations, we come to an understanding of things; by thinking about our actions, we create a rational coherence in our lives. And we know that we are only worthily fulfilling our tasks as human beings when we let ourselves be guided by the right thoughts, both in knowing and in acting. Therefore, the human soul faces a dual necessity. Out of natural necessity, it is governed by the laws of the body, but because it freely recognizes their necessity it also allows itself to be governed by the laws that lead to correct thinking. Nature subjects us to the laws of metabolism, but as human beings we subject ourselves to the laws of thought."

"Theosophy" – Chapter 1 – Rudolf Steiner

https://wn.rsarchive.org/Books/GA009/English/AP1971/GA009_c01.html

Steiner goes into great detail to give us the make-up of the human being in this and many other of his works.

Foundational Flows

It is with this idea of the 3-fold nature of the soul that we start our investigation of the birth chart to find the symbols to construct our foundational level work toward the synching of flow between soul and spirit. This 3-fold soul nature is to be thought of as consisting of the 3 following functions of consciousness:

1) Thinking
2) Feeling
3) Willing

At a core level these are the 3 basic soul functions. In an evolutionary way of thinking these 3 functions are in a process of transformation into higher, more specific variations of those 3 functions. This is done over vast epochs of time and is one of the reasons for reincarnation, to gather new experience as the ground for our conscious evolution. Steiner describes these evolutionary epochs of time and within each the focus is upon a specific evolving aspect of our being. These time periods are equated with Astrological and Cultural Ages of 2,160 years. The Astrological age starts and then there is a time-lag of almost 1,200 years when the Cultural age catches up and begins. This 1,200-year lag is based upon the transformation of consciousness and is related to the Venus cycle. For more on this in detail see - Robert Powell – "Hermetic Astrology" Volume 1 – Chapter 3.

https://www.fieldsbooks.com/cgi-bin/fields/cpg/sophiafoundation

Astrological Ages	Dates
Cancer	8426 - 6266 BC
Gemini	6266 - 4106 BC
Taurus	4106 - 1946 BC
Aries	1946 BC - 215 AD
Pisces	215 - 2375 AD
Aquarius	2375 - 4535 AD

Astrological Ages

Astrological ages are determined by the regression of the vernal point through the signs of the zodiac. Cultural ages start after a time-lag of about 1,200 years after the start of the Astrological age.

Cultural Age	Dates	Part of Human being developed
Ancient Indian	7227 - 5067 BC	Etheric body
Ancient Indian	5067 - 2907 BC	Sentient body
Ancient Egyptian	2907 - 747 BC	Sentient soul
Greco - Roman	747 BC - 1414 AD	Intellectual or Mind soul
Present Age	1414 - 3574 AD	Consciousness soul
6th Age	3574 - 5734 AD	Manas (Spirit Self)
7th Age	5734 - 7894 AD	Budhi (Life Spirit)

Post - Atlantean Cultural Ages

Foundational Flows

At the most basic level we describe thinking, feeling and willing as the 3 foundational soul qualities. We will be looking at them now as being represented by three astrological symbols from the natal chart.

    Thinking – Mercury – ☿

    Feeling – Venus - ♀

    Willing – Mars – ♂

Arguments will be made that feeling is a Moon (☽) function. In another work we will go into that in much greater detail. It is certainly connected with the nervous system, sensation and the karmic predisposition for the automatic coloring and bias of that sensation. But the actual conscious soul function at the level of feeling we are dealing with here has a Venus (♀) gesture.

These are the positions we work with at the foundational level to come up with organ flow patterns from Jin Shin Jyutsu to assist in flow between soul and spirit. Beyond this foundational level, flows are chosen from other natal planetary positions, which correspond to the more evolved soul functions that we have already attained and or/are currently working on in this epoch.

At this point we can only say that these (Mercury, Venus and Mars) are the planetary symbols used at the foundational level. Before we can go on to show how they are determined at a soul and then Higher Self level of association we need to talk a bit about the different kinds of 'zodiacs'.

Chapter 4
Zodiacal differentiations and associations

The zodiac is the starry background to the apparent path of the Sun across the celestial sphere over the course of the year. The orbits of the Moon and planets also lie entirely within this belt of stars or constellations, of which there are 12. This belt extends 9⁰ on either side of the ecliptic, the plane of the Earth's orbit.

There are different 'zodiacs' used in astrology. These differing zodiacs give us different perspectives and orientations. These different orientations then also yield insights into the various aspects of our being. The fact that this is true is based upon the ancient hermetic axiom, "As Above, So Below".

The first zodiac we will consider is the Tropical zodiac which is currently the most widely used in the western world. It is based upon a certain interpretation of Ptolemy's writings which places 0⁰ Aries (♈) as starting on the first day of spring.

The second zodiac is the Sidereal zodiac and is based upon the starry background that we experience when we look up at the night sky. These star groups, or constellations, are this 12-fold group which the paths of the Sun, Moon and planets would be seen to have as their background relative to a viewer on Earth. This is the zodiac more widely used in eastern astrology.

Both of these examples are known as geocentric perspectives since they are Earth-centered, taking the viewer as centered upon the Earth as the premise. There are arguments in favor of both. The Tropical is season-based, or determined by the calendar. It has even been argued that it represents the 'life-body' of Earth. This perspective is certainly useful in determining the psychological make-up of our personality. It will here be used as representing the psychological level of the personality-level conditioned ego. This can be imagined as a Lunar (☽) level of reflecting karmic and environmental conditioning which gives the personality its psychological basis.

Foundational Flows

The geocentric Sidereal chart will here be used to determine a more soul level understanding of the individual. Sidereal means 'stars', and the soul body is called the 'astral' body which means star body. So again we see "As Above, So Below." This can be thought to represent a more Solar (☉) level of our being as opposed to the personality or Lunar (☽) level.

The difference between the two geocentric zodiacs is currently about 25^0 which is due to the precession of the equinoxes. This is due to a wobble in the Earth's axis of rotation which creates a large variation in the course of an almost 26,000 year cycle.

Approximately 2,000 years ago the two zodiacs were aligned and now the precession has them offset by 25^0. This difference 'regresses', at a rate of almost 1^0 every 72 years, backward through the constellations.

Now we must introduce a third perspective with the Heliocentric Sidereal chart. This is a constellation-based chart (sidereal) but from the perspective of the Sun (☉) at the center instead of the Earth. It is used with the same birth time as any other natal chart but it gives us more clues to the perspective of our spirit, specifically, as it is called, our Higher Self.

Here are the three perspectives we are now considering –

1) Geocentric Tropical natal chart — conditioned ego at personality level
2) Geocentric Sidereal natal chart — soul level considerations
3) Heliocentric Sidereal natal chart — Higher Self level considerations

If we follow through with these ideas we will circle back to where we started in our discussion of astrology. Let us look at the wheel of the horoscope again. In discussing the trinity of Sun, Moon and Ascendant I mentioned the Ascendant as the Eastern horizon point, the Rising point (sign). Here is what was said, "It helps us emphasize our particular relationship to the world. The wheel of the horoscope, divided into 12 houses, represents our particular relationship to the inner and outer world. We can see the Ascendant as our own personalized way that we are oriented to this wheel of life."

Foundational Flows

The spirit germ comes from the periphery, as formative forces from the 12 constellations. This becomes the expression of the 'I'. On January 1, 1921 Rudolf Steiner said, "We're studying reality only when we study on the one hand the starry skies and on the other hand the development of the embryo…what happens in the cell should be conceived in the following way…let us consider it in its most common form, namely the spherical form…But what is the spherical form? The thin fluid mass is still left entirely to its own devices, and therefore it behaves according to impulses received from its surroundings. What does it do? Well, it mirrors the universe around it! It takes on the form of the sphere because it mirrors in miniature the whole cosmos, which we imagine initially in the ideal form of a sphere."

This coming into manifest form from the planetary spheres and the starry realms is guided by divine wisdom and the help of the spiritual hierarchies. Once we take our first breath, Steiner tells us the starry realms are at that moment imprinted even into the structure of our brains. The wheel of the horoscope and its 12 divisions also reflect this mirroring and now our physical life is played out in the mirroring of this structure in both our inner and outer life experiences. These are the experiences of our 'I'.

In "Why on Earth? Biography and the Practice of Becoming Human", Signe Eklund Schaefer states, in the section on 'Finding ourselves through others', "It would be a misinterpretation…to assume that while we are experiencing ourselves between death and a new birth, we are the sole planner of our future earthly journey, that somehow on our own we plot out our best next trip. The picture that Steiner gives is of an interaction between our higher 'I', wise spiritual beings and the 'others' who are part of our story. Later, as we live our days on earth, we discover aspects of ourselves in meeting the invitations to our becoming offered by the others of our life. Our 'I' is not held tightly within us, nor does it somehow hover above us trying to direct our self-appointed actions. Rather, it lives in the people and circumstances we meet; it waits to be incorporated, to be taken up by us, to be allowed to develop in ever-new ways."

This is expressed in the horoscope through our experiences of the houses as revealing our hidden 'I'.

This 'I', then is also revealed in its many levels of expression through the different zodiacs, and the associated charts that we have shown. See the table above again showing Tropical geocentric as representing our conditioned ego, 'I', at the personality level. The Sidereal geocentric is the soul level expression of our 'I' and Heliocentric is the Higher Self expression of the 'I'.

This is why we are seeking out our Foundational Flows. We are looking for a way to assist the 'flow' between these different octaves of expression of the 'I'. We are looking for a way to help ourselves consciously evolve.

Chapter 5
Harmonizing soul and spirit with flow

Now we can start looking at the different charts and the relationships between them. With the focus now being on the harmonizing of soul and spirit we can consider what planetary players are involved and how we can take advantage of these relationships.

We will be using the 3 planets discussed above, Mercury, Venus and Mars as representing the basic functional soul qualities of thinking, feeling and willing. We will be comparing the positions of these 3 planets in the various types of zodiacal charts to help us find the relationships we will be trying to help synch the flow between soul and spirit.

The very first comparison is between the Tropical and Sidereal Geocentric charts. This is the most basic starting point and can be considered as the difference between the personality and soul level 'projects' in a thinking, feeling and willing way.

As will be discussed and explained later this is just a beginning relationship that we start working with. Especially for someone already working on their spiritual path, it may only be needed for a few sessions in the beginning. This is because the real level of flow that we are seeking to work on is shown in the 'projects' revealed in the relationship between the sidereal geocentric and heliocentric charts. This is then reflecting those 'projects' that have to do with the relationship of the soul and Higher Self. Keep in mind that Steiner pointed out that all of the spiritual hierarchies are always evolving, so the expressions of these symbols as 'projects' are certainly an appropriate way of looking at them even from this perspective of the Higher Self.

Let us look at some chart examples to discover these positions —

Foundational Flows

♀ - Venus

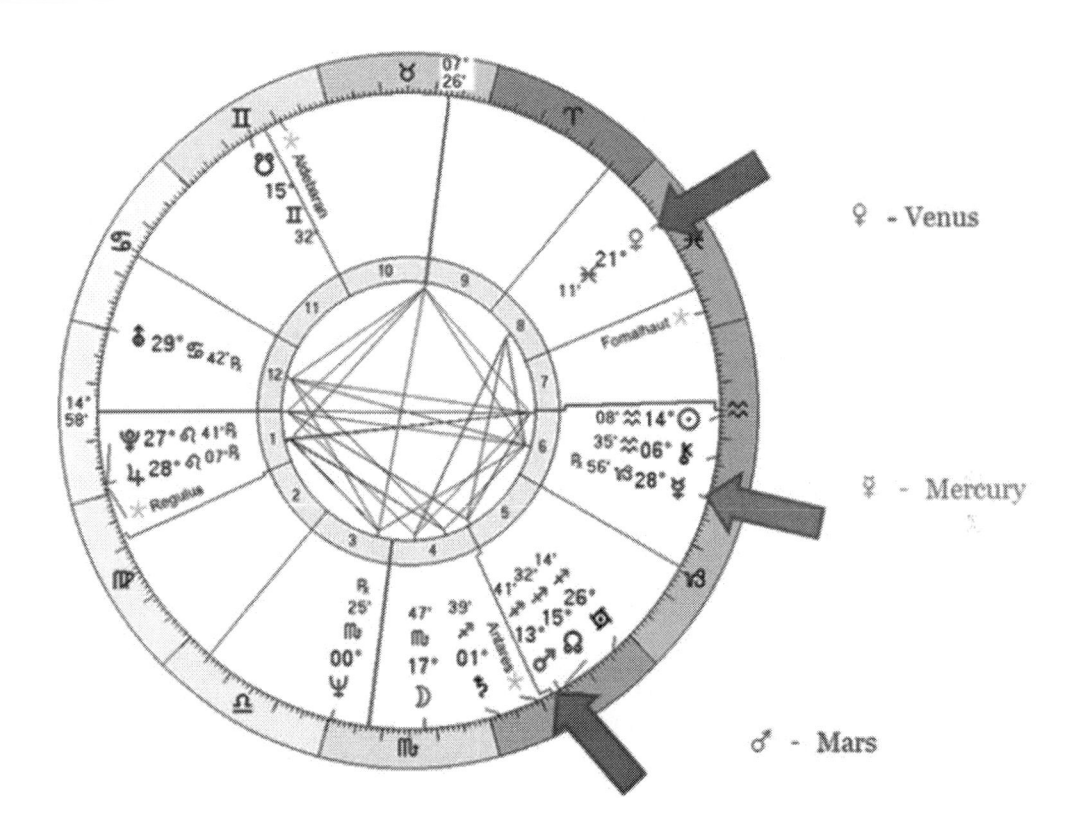

☿ - Mercury

♂ - Mars

Above we see the Tropical geocentric zodiac with Mercury (☿) in Capricorn (♑), Venus (♀) in Pisces (♓) and Mars (♂) in Sagittarius (♐).

Foundational Flows

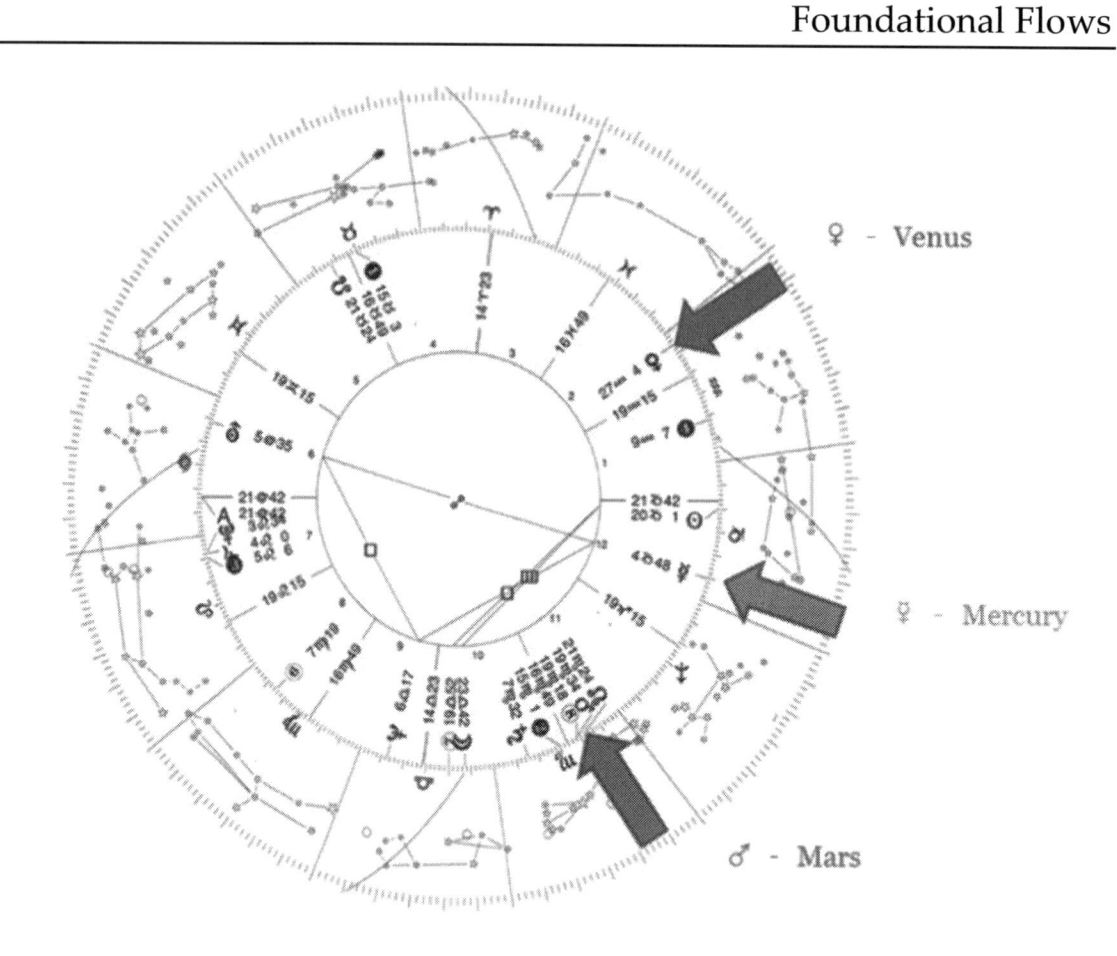

Here we see the Sidereal geocentric zodiac with Mercury (☿) in Capricorn (♑), Venus (♀) in Aquarius (♒) and Mars (♂) in Scorpio (♏) with the starry background of the constellations shown.

Foundational Flows

♀ - Venus

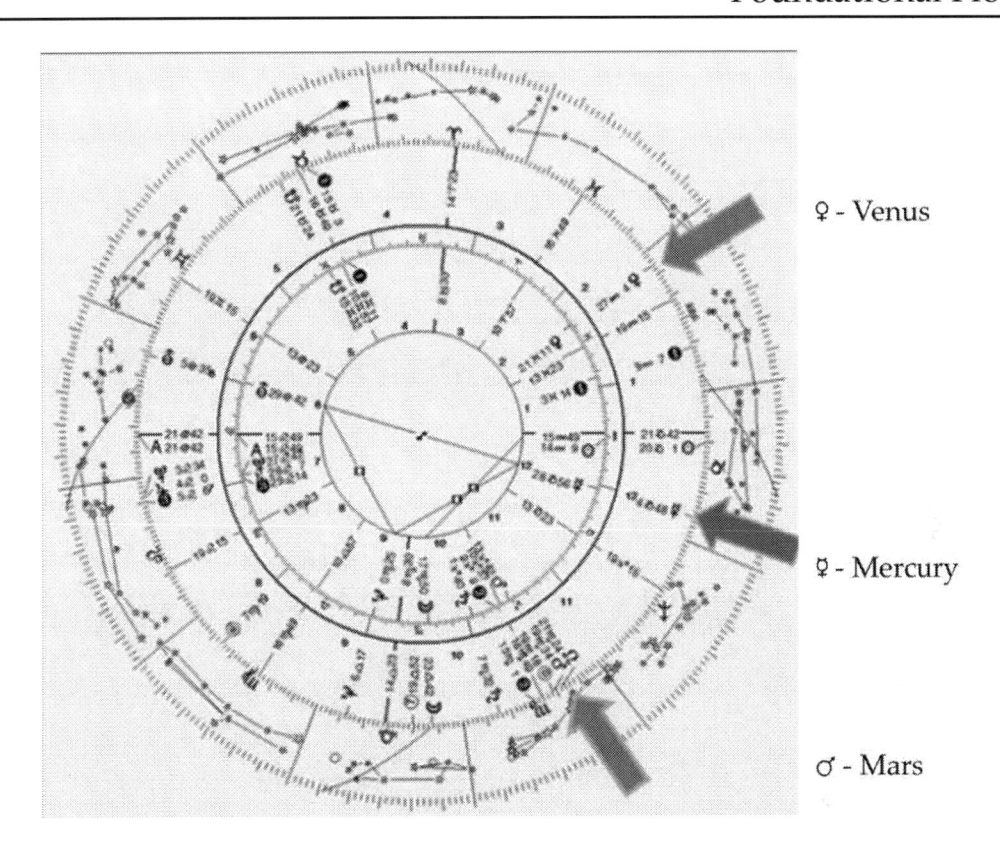

☿ - Mercury

♂ - Mars

Here we see the 2 charts, Tropical (inner) and Sidereal (outer), compared within the starry background. We see the same relative positions of the planets in both wheels. By this I mean for you to see that within the wheels that the positions of all the planets are at the same place in each wheel. What is then noticeable is that the 'signs' of many of the planets are different between the wheels.

Now we clearly see the 25 degree difference between tropical sign and sidereal constellation designations.

Foundational Flows

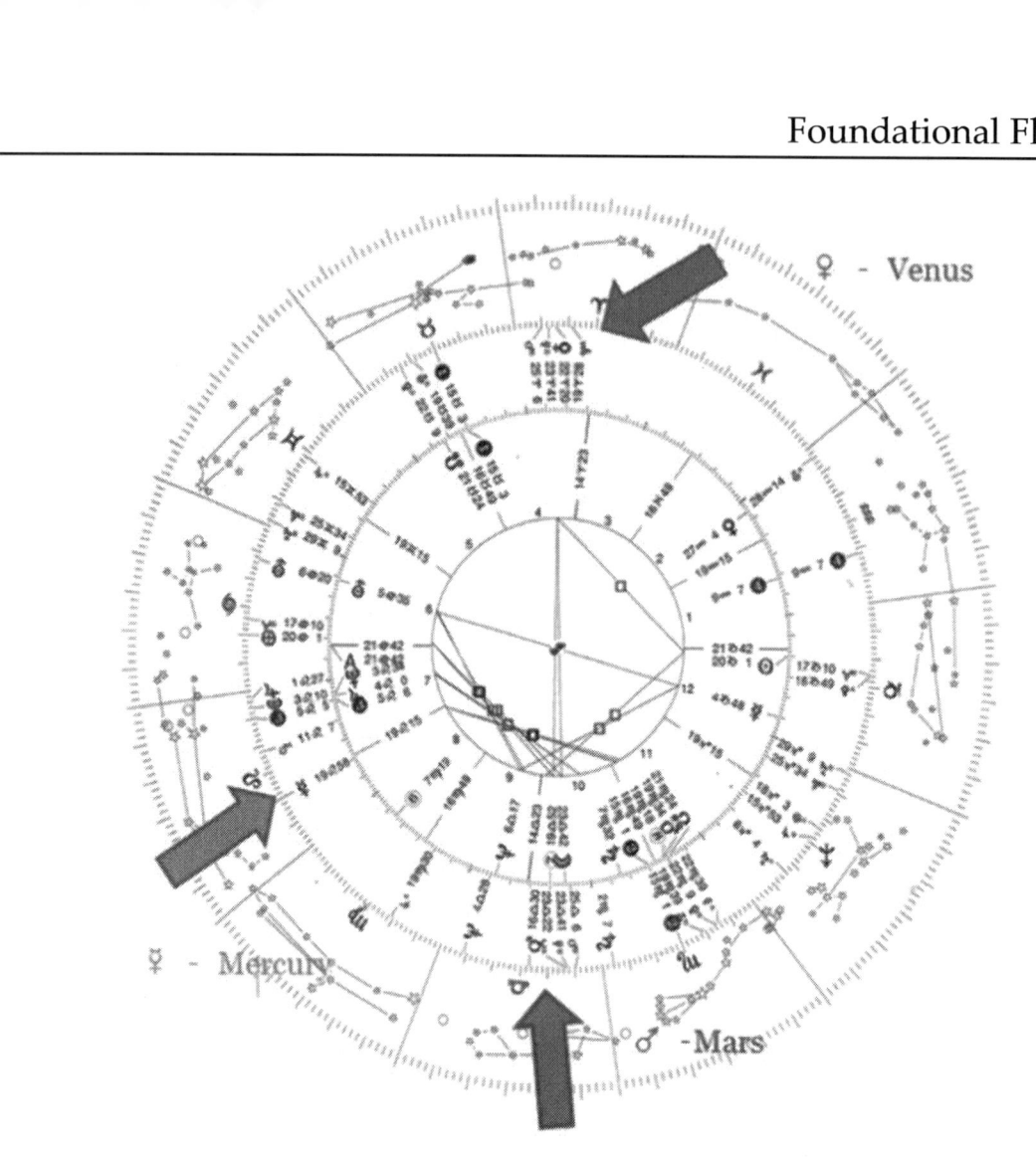

Here we see in the outer wheel the Sidereal zodiac with Heliocentric Mercury (☿) in Leo (♌), Venus (♀) in Aries (♈) and Mars (♂) in Libra (♎). This is added to the inner wheel Sidereal geocentric chart. Notice what 3 main things have moved between these two wheels.

Foundational Flows

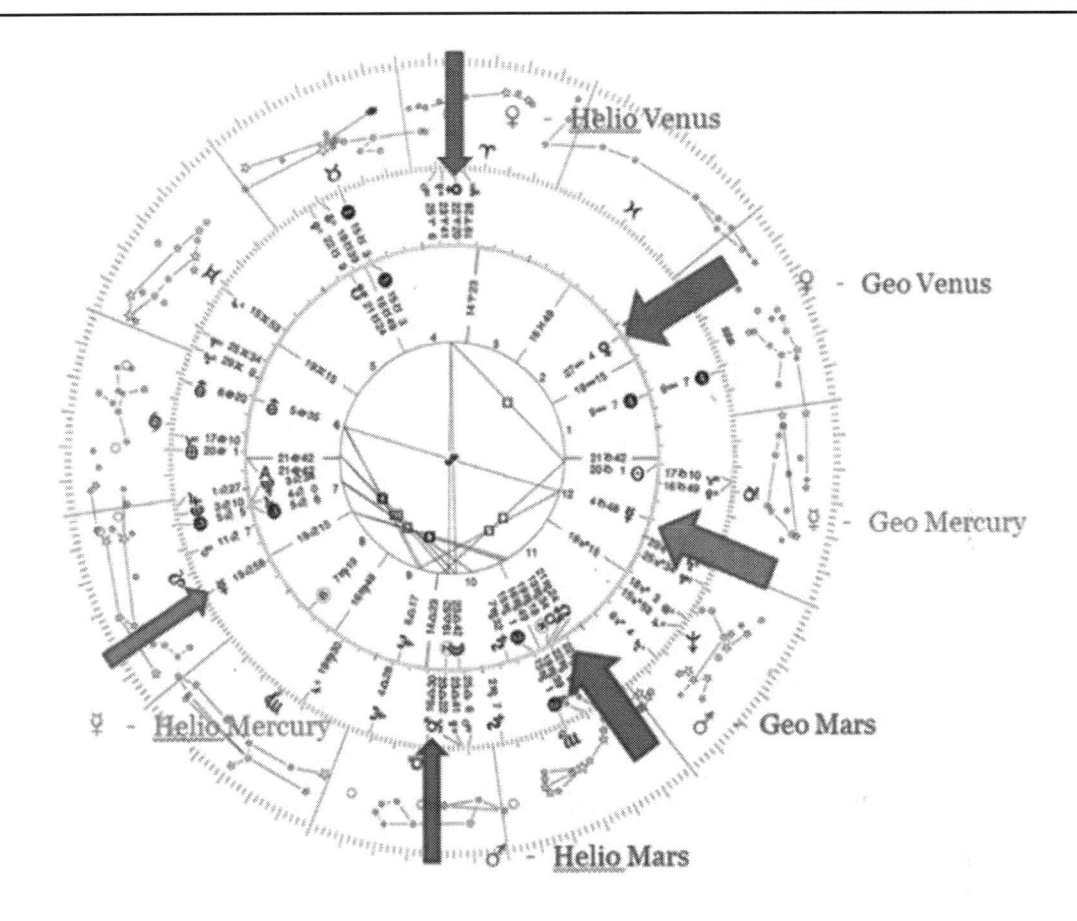

Here we see in the inner wheel the Sidereal Geocentric and outer wheel Heliocentric positions as before, but now labeled separately.

Now we have shown examples of all the chart combinations that we are looking for in our Foundational level of harmonizing the flow of soul and spirit to assist in their optimal communication and cooperation.

As we notice in this comparison chart the geocentric positions of the inner planets – Mercury, Venus and Mars – have shifted their positions considerably in the Heliocentric chart. Sometimes they shift radically and sometimes little if at all.

Foundational Flows

Also note that the outer planets shift less and less as we move further out. This again hints at more of a generational and collective influence with the outer planets and to higher aspects of our being as well.

In our next chapter we will show the organ flow pattern associations for each of our examples. Then we will show how to combine them in useful ways for organ flow pattern support, Self-Help finger sequences and the deeper meaning behind this harmonizing of flow.

Chapter 6
Finding the Organ Flow patterns to be used as derived from the natal chart

In our first example we showed a Geocentric Tropical natal chart. In that chart we found that Mercury was in Capricorn, Venus was in Pisces and Mars was in Sagittarius.

If we go back to our Tables showing the organ flow pattern correspondences, we then have the following –

Thinking	Mercury (☿)	Capricorn (♑)	Umbilicus Flow
Feeling	Venus (♀)	Pisces (♓)	Liver Flow
Willing	Mars (♂)	Sagittarius (♐)	Diaphragm Flow

This gives us the organ flow patterns for the 'projects' indicated for this incarnation on the personality level.

In our second example we showed a Geocentric Sidereal natal chart. In this chart we found that Mercury was still in Capricorn, Venus was in Aquarius and Mars was in Scorpio.

If we go back to our Tables showing the organ flow pattern correspondences, we then have the following –

Thinking	Mercury (☿)	Capricorn (♑)	Umbilicus Flow
Feeling	Venus (♀)	Aquarius (♒)	Gall Bladder Flow
Willing	Mars (♂)	Scorpio (♏)	Kidney Flow

This gives us the organ flow patterns for the 'projects' indicated for this incarnation on the soul level.

Foundational Flows

Now for our first level session, to get flow 'kick-started', we use this relationship of 'projects' as indicated between the positions in the 2 natal charts. The 'relationship' here is between the conditioned ego at the personality level and the soul level. This relationship will be expressive of any evolutionary tension that exists in this incarnation.

The Tropical, conditioned personality level ego, 'projects' which are referring to Thinking, Feeling and Willing on that level need to be synched up with the same soul level symbols from the Sidereal chart.

We only need to do a few of these sessions if the person has in any way already been doing conscious work along their own personal spiritual path. I am at least introducing this level of harmonizing these functions as more of a 'kick-start' to the overall process.

The way the sessions are done is explained in the next chapter. First let us practice finding the organ flow pattern correspondences for our other chart example.

In our third example we showed a Heliocentric Sidereal natal chart. In this chart we found that Mercury was in Leo, Venus was in Aries and Mars was in Libra.

If we go back to our Tables showing the organ flow pattern correspondences, we then have the following –

Thinking	Mercury (☿)	Leo (♌)	Heart Flow
Feeling	Venus (♀)	Aries (♈)	Lung Flow
Willing	Mars (♂)	Libra (♎)	Urinary Bladder Flow

This gives us the organ flow patterns for the 'projects' indicated for this incarnation relative to the Higher Self level.

Now we have seen how to derive the organ flow patterns from the charts and planetary positions that correspond to the Foundational level used in this harmonizing of flow between soul and spirit. Next, we will see how to use these flows to help accomplish this aim.

Chapter 7
How to use the Foundational Flows

The ideal usage of organ flow patterns in this method requires two practitioners working together on a third individual whose flows have been determined. This will be called a 'triad' of people at the table. Each practitioner actually does a 'triad' of flows within one session. This will be described as follows –

For demonstration purposes we might designate the Tropical geocentric chart as chart 'A', and the Sidereal geocentric chart as chart 'B'. We then set up such that the person on the right side of the body is doing the triad of flows from chart A. The person seated to the left of the body receiving is using the triad of flows from chart B. In Jin Shin Jyutsu the right side is feminine and the left is masculine, so if the practitioners happen to be a male and a female they may sit accordingly, although this is certainly not a hard and fast rule. I encourage intuition and creativity everywhere within this method that seems allowable to the individuals involved.

With the two practitioners seated on either side they begin doing the 'two-sided flows' simultaneously. They each begin with the Mars (σ) position flows on both sides of the body. As they complete these organ flow patterns, they then move into the next organ flow patterns corresponding with the Venus ($♀$) position derived from each chart. Lastly, they will do the Mercury ($☿$) position organ flow patterns simultaneously until completed. This means doing the 'Willing' flows simultaneously, then the 'Feeling' flows simultaneously and then the same with the 'Thinking' flows.

The session should not take longer than an hour in total. This means using 15 – 20 minutes for each set of these triad flows corresponding to Willing, Feeling and Thinking. I will go into more detail on the reasoning for the order of the flows later in this presentation.

Foundational Flows

Let us diagram how the above description might look, using the example charts already presented.

Right side of body	*Left side of body*
Chart A – Personality Level	Chart B – Soul Level
Tropical Geocentric Flows	Sidereal Geocentric Flows
1) Willing Level — Mars (♂)	
Sagittarius (♐) — Diaphragm	Scorpio (♏) — Kidney
2) Feeling Level — Venus (♀)	
Pisces (♓) — Liver	Aquarius (♒) — Gall Bladder
3) Thinking Level — Mercury (☿)	
Capricorn (♑) — Umbilicus	Capricorn (♑) — Umbilicus

The next example will be of our Foundational Flows level of harmonizing soul and spirit.

Right side of body	*Left side of body*
Chart B – Soul Level	Chart C – Higher Self
Sidereal Geocentric Flows	Sidereal Heliocentric Flows
1) Willing Level — Mars (♂)	
Scorpio (♏) — Kidney	Libra (♎) — Urinary Bladder
2) Feeling Level — Venus (♀)	
Aquarius (♒) — Gall Bladder	Aries (♈) — Lung
3) Thinking Level — Mercury (☿)	
Capricorn (♑) — Umbilicus	Leo (♌) — Heart

Foundational Flows

So, we can now see how we are combining and using the 3 different zodiac charts – Tropical geocentric, Sidereal geocentric and Sidereal Heliocentric – to synch, with Flow, the relationships that exist between the 3 levels of our Being that we have been discussing.

When we do the organ flow patterns of Jin Shin Jyutsu we are not just addressing the physical body. We are not just working with the physiology. These organ function energies are working through a functional weaving that courses throughout every layer of our Being. This gets expressed most obviously when it is expressing a dysfunction. When we are not in Flow it is not just expressed in our physiology, but also in our entire consciousness, as expressed in our Thinking, Feeling and Willing.

These 'relationships' may exist in more or less tension as revealed through our 'projects' and 'attitudes'. Remember that 'we are first and foremost spiritual Beings' and 'Flow' is the KEY to a harmoniously functioning experiencing of our Being. Using these Foundational Flows helps us be able to focus in on the precise 'relationships' that need the most 'attending' in any individual. This 'attending' on the 3 primary levels is expressed in Jin Shin Jyutsu as Physio-Philosophy, Physio-Psychology and Physio-Physiology. This 3-folding is expressed throughout our daily living, as 'spiritual Beings having a bodily experience'.

The question is, 'Do we experience this in a Flowing way, or not?'

Chapter 8
A word about the sessions – timing and frequency

It is ideal to have a triad of people to do this method. But it is not the only possible way. If there are only two people, one giving the session and one receiving, it can still be accomplished. The one giving the session just needs to do all six flows. Mars organ flow patterns will be done first beginning with left side then right. Then the Venus organ flow patterns and Mercury organ flow patterns after that, done the same way.

This means that the person being the jumper-cable is doing six flows back to back within the one hour time allowed for the session. Now we divide the hour by six instead of three. The allotted time becomes a little less than ten minutes per flow. In this situation one might want to receive the sessions a little more often and for a longer series of sessions, but the ultimate outcome should remain the same. And remember to give the person their individualized Self-Help finger sequence to do daily as well to continue the effect.

Ideally, again, perhaps in a retreat setting, the receiver would receive a session once or twice daily for 5 – 7 days in a row. If this ideal were being met one could do the synching of chart A and Chart B the first day and follow with the Foundational level sessions by synching chart B with Chart C the remainder of the sessions and days. We have done the Foundational Flows in this type of situation and setting many times and it truly is transformative.

Repeating the Foundational level sessions in a series like this can be repeated as often as is feasible. Then there will come a time when it will be appropriate to move on to the flows of the next levels which will be covered in Volume 2 of this work.

Chapter 9
The Fly in the Ointment - Astral vs Etheric Body

At this point we have shown how to use the planets Mercury, Venus and Mars (representing Thinking, Feeling and Willing) which we find in the Geocentric Sidereal birth chart and then also in the Heliocentric version. We showed how to find the corresponding Jin Shin Jyutsu organ flow patterns which we then use as our Fundamental Flows. It is in combining these organ flow patterns between the charts that we are synching up the relationship between soul and spirit. We showed that we do the Willing organ flow patterns together to harmonize that level first. Then we do the same for the Feeling and then also the Thinking organ flow patterns which we have derived from the two charts. I think now is an appropriate time to show why we are emphasizing the sidereal charts in this work and only using the Tropical natal chart in the beginning.

Our premise is that the Tropical chart emphasizes the personality level conditioned ego. Johnathan Hilton describes the tropical zodiac as "born out of the seasonal, yearly life of the earth...the tropical signs are a zodiac of the life realm of the Earth, the etheric realm." https://www.astrosophy.com/

Adrian Anderson, as Damien Pryor, emphasizes the importance of the tropical zodiac in "psychological profiling" and even names it an 'Inherent Zodiac' equating it with an "energy field surrounding the Earth's upper atmosphere" as an "integral part of our planet's life system." https://www.rudolfsteinerstudies.com/

So why do we emphasize the Sidereal zodiac in this work? Especially if the Tropical zodiac represents the 'life body'? Wouldn't we want to strengthen the life body of the person?

The answer is, Yes, we DO want to strengthen the 'life body' of the person. Now we just have to understand the best way to do that.

We are using the Sidereal zodiac as the zodiac that most represents the soul level. Sidereal means 'stars", astral means "stars". Using the "As Above, So Below" comparison we see what Ageless Wisdom has been pointing to. Another name for the soul body is the astral body, the star body. The Sidereal zodiac is comprised of the 12 star constellations through which the Sun has its apparent motion; it is the forces coming from the constellations that are reflected in our soul body.

So, we have one zodiac which represents our life body and another that represents our soul body. In Robert Powell's work, 'Hermetic Astrology', he shows that the sidereal zodiac is the correct one to use in reincarnation research by using example charts of individuals Steiner indicated to be such reincarnating souls. Powell shows that the sidereal zodiac holds up in the examples Steiner gave over long periods of time and that the tropical zodiac does not.

Expanding on this important differentiation between life body and astral body, there is another important clue given by Dennis Klocek. Citing Rudolf Steiner's "The Fundamentals of Therapy", he gives Steiner's example of the 'inflammation process'.

"The old terminology for the phases of inflammation were:

> **Calor** - heat
>
> **Rubor** - red
>
> **Tumor** – hardening
>
> **Dolor** - pain

So in that process, Calor, Rubor, Tumor - an inflammation leads to a tumor forming, a hardening.

When the hardening happens and the pain comes that's actually a sign that the whole inflammatory processes is unfolding in a healing direction.

So inflammation, even though it could kill you, is a healing process, a natural healing process.

Foundational Flows

And sclerosis is the opposite pole to inflammation. Technically sclerosis means depositing something or hardening something. So that the Tumor in Calor, Rubor, Tumor and Dolor - Tumor is sclerosis and depositing.

And in healing processes, or in the growth of the body in general, the forming of a bone, the forming of a tissue out of the fluid, is a sclerotic process. We could call the forming of tissue out of fluid, growth. But, it's sclerotic technically.

So sclerosis, which is considered to be a disease process, is actually a natural process in the body.

So inflammation, as from an infection that could kill you, and sclerosis are both actually natural healing forces in the body.

Steiner mentions that and says 'So, where does the illness come in?'

It's a really good question and the answer he gives is that the illness is not in the body and the life forces. The illness is in thoughts we bring to the body and the life forces. The illness is in the soul.

And that picture is… what we could call the 'body-mind connection'. The soul and the interaction of the soul forces, the forces of consciousness, interacting with the forces of life, creates a condition of tension - because in Steiner's point of view, the forces of consciousness, the force of the ego, IS the source of disease.

This is a very sobering thought, but it's at the heart of the revolution that Steiner brought to the medical work. It's that the pole of consciousness is the disease producing vector, it is the disease vector. It's not a germ.

The soul process creates a potential for the germ to find a milieu in which it can multiply… consciousness is the disease vector…

It's what he then calls the 'fly in the ointment'."

Dennis Klocek – Esoteric Physiology lecture series - https://dennisklocek.com

So we can see from this that it is never the life body that causes illness, its whole gesture is growth and reproduction. It is the consciousness of the 'I' at the soul level that we need to harmonize and work with in order to re-establish flow and healthy physiology at all levels of our being. It is consciousness that restrains the free flowing power of the life forces through 'attitudes' which reflect our karmic 'projects'.

The 'I' is the bridge that manifests between the 3 worlds – physical, soul and spirit worlds – in its various octaves of manifestation. These different octaves of manifestation in these 3 worlds are as 1) - the conditioned personality level ego or 'I', 2) - the soul level consciousness, or 'I', and 3) - the Higher Self level of consciousness, or 'I'.

These are all octaves of expression of our 'True Self', or 'I AM'. These aspects of the 'I AM' and its various octaves of manifestation are detailed more fully in another project. But it is the vast works of Rudolf Steiner that most fully detail these relationships.

This brings in the next part of our equation.

"The human being consists of body, soul and spirit. The human body is subject to the laws of heredity, the human soul to the laws of karma, and the human spirit is subject to the laws of reincarnation."

- Rudolf Steiner – "Theosophy"

https://wn.rsarchive.org/Books/GA009/English/AP1971/GA009_c01.html

Repeating - It is consciousness that restrains the free flowing power of the life forces through 'attitudes' which reflect our karmic 'projects'.

As Trevor Ravenscroft points out in, "The Cup of Destiny", it was Buddha who taught 'The Four Noble Truths' and brought us 'The Eightfold Path'.

"The First Truth is the existence of suffering in the world, especially the suffering of birth and death. The suffering of separation from those we love and the inability to acquire and maintain that which we desire.

Foundational Flows

The Second Truth addresses the cause of suffering. The cause of suffering is "from the fact that the 'thirst for existence' insinuates itself into man. This is from the results of his deeds in former incarnations. Man is characterized by ignorance, his blindness to what he has brought over from a previous earth life which has now become an integral part of him. Because of his lack of perception, everything which confronts him from evil powers in the universe, and which he would otherwise ward off, has been transformed into a thirst for existence. Man's thinking has developed out of this craving for life and this is why people are quite unable to think objectively…

Buddha made a fine distinction between objective thinking, which has nothing but the object in view, and the type of thinking influenced by personal desire. Everything acquired as only an apparent truth - not as the result of objective thought, but because old inclinations have been brought from previous lives on earth - forms <u>a hidden organ of inclination</u>. This organ of inclination comprises the sum total of the way a man thinks because of certain experiences in former incarnations.

This hidden organ of inclination even affects the sense organs. It is especially influential in the eye. Hence the eye does not see with pure vision. It would look into the outer world quite differently if it were not inwardly permeated with the residue of karma from earlier lives. The result is that there is mingled into all things the desire to see this or that, hear this or that, taste this or that or perceive in one way or another…

The Third Noble Truth of the Buddha concerns the manner in which suffering is eliminated in the world: by eliminating its cause; by extinguishing the thirst for existence which has arisen through ignorance.

Men have lost their original *dull* clairvoyance …Men have as a result become ignorant because the great macrocosm of spiritual beings has been concealed from them. This ignorance is to blame for the thirst for existence which in turn has caused pain, toil and death."

The remedy includes reawakening to our spiritual inheritance, but now on a self-conscious level. What Trevor calls the 'original dull clairvoyance' - through

Foundational Flows

which we experienced ourselves as one with the spiritual world – must now be reacquired but in a new transformed way. It has to be developed from a new sense of self-conscious awareness. This is the new metamorphosis which the 'I' must partake through conscious soul work. This is what is meant by the marriage of soul and spirit, harmonizing flow between these parts of our being so that we can be awakened by the kiss of consciousness from the Higher Self.

"Now I want you to consider… that everything there is by way of stars in the sky has a definite influence on the earth as a whole and specifically also on the human being. We truly depend not only on what exists here on earth but also on the stars that are there in the heavens.

Think of some star or constellation up there. It rises in the evening, as we say, and sets in the morning. It is there all the time, and always influences the human being. But think of another constellation, the Twins, let us say, or the Lion. The moon passes that way. The moment it passes that way it covers up the Twins or the Lion… At that moment they cannot influence the earth, because their influence is blocked. And so we have stars everywhere in the sky that are never blocked out, neither by the sun nor by the moon, and always have an influence on the earth. And we have stars which the moon passes, and the sun seemingly also passes them. These are covered up from time to time and their influence then stops. We are therefore able to say that the Lion is a constellation in the zodiac and has a particular influence on the human being. It does not have this influence if the moon is in front of it. At that time the human being is free of the Lion influence, the Lion's influence does not affect him…

Human beings need these influences…It has this influence for as long as it is not covered up by the moon or the sun…then you have to find the power in yourself.

The Lion continually influences human beings except when it is covered by the moon. Then the influence is not there. When the moon blocks the Lion's influence, the human being must develop using his own resources. Someone able to develop his own strong Lion influence when the moon covers the constellation may thus be called a Lion person. Someone able to develop particularly the influence in the constellation of the Crab when this is covered up is a Crab person. People develop the one or the other more strongly depending on their inner constitution.

You see, therefore, that the constellations of the zodiac are special, for with them, the influence is sometimes there and sometimes not. The moon, passing through the constellations at four-week intervals, brings it about that there is always a time in a four week period when some constellation of the zodiac does not have an influence. With other constellations the influence is always the same. In earlier times people took these influences that came from the heavens very seriously. The zodiac was therefore more important to them than other constellations. The others have a continuous influence which does not change. But with the zodiac we may say that the influence changes depending on whether one of its constellations is covered over or not. Because of this, the influence of the zodiac on the earth has always been the subject of special study. And so you see why the zodiac is more important when we study the starry heavens than other stars are."

Rudolf Steiner – Dornach, May 17, 1924

"Before our rebirth we are connected with the entire starry universe.

The unique relationship of an individual to the cosmic system determines which forces lead them back to earth; they also determine to which parents and to which locality we are brought. The impulse to incarnate in one place or another, in this or that family, in this or that nation, at this or that point in time, is determined by the way the individual is integrated in the cosmos before birth.... People who are knowledgeable about these things can 'read' the forces that determine a person's path in her or his physical life; on this basis horoscopes are cast. Each of us is assigned a particular horoscope, in which the forces are revealed that have led us into this life. For example, if in a particular horoscope Mars is over Aries, this means that certain Aries forces cannot pass through Mars but are weakened instead.

Thus, human beings on their way into physical existence can get their bearings through their horoscope."

- Rudolf Steiner – June 8, 1911

Now we must put these pieces together. The soul is the "fly in the ointment", consciousness is the disease vector. Consciousness, or soul, is the level we need to work with to enable the possibility of harmonizing to take place. Remember the soul is the sleeping princess waiting to be awakened with the kiss of consciousness by the Higher Self. It is not the life body that we need to try and directly work with. What we need to do is release the hindering influences of the karmically skewed consciousness that is blocking the full flow of the life forces. There is soul work that is required in order to be prepared to receive this kiss of awakening. In other words, we have to be consciously engaged throughout this process.

Along with the soul work which we must do on our chosen spiritual path we can now add our individually determined Foundational Flows. These are the organ flow patterns that correspond to the positions of Mercury, Venus and Mars (Thinking, Feeling and Willing). By their position they represent the organ flow patterns that correspond to the 'projects' we are coming in to work with. These positions in the chart reflect the filters of consciousness which are karmically determined and biased. They help us to understand the karmic 'organ of inclination' which colors our experience.

And Rudolf Steiner said that the positions occupied by the planets block the full expression of the forces of the background constellation of stars and are therefore weakened.

We need to consciously return to the 'essence level' of flow which has been hindered in its full functioning by our emphasis on living life from the 'attitude' level. By working to unblock the flow we return to our intended functional level. Working with the soul to build a bridge to the Higher Self is the solution. Flow in our entire Being is the goal.

Foundational Flows

This is our final clue – the constellation thus blocked gives us the answer as to which organ flow pattern is weakened. It is weakened because the cosmic stream of forces coming from the starry periphery was weakened, blocked. We can see these positions as the representing a functional gesture of synchronistic expression that mirrors our inner and outer experience of life based on our past incarnational karmic coloring.

And by using these associated organ flow patterns from Jin Shin Jyutsu as our Foundational Flows we can then strengthen the very weaknesses and restraints which we came in with and which are our 'projects'. These 'projects' are expressions of the hindering influence of consciousness on our life force body. Harmonizing them with the flows found in the Heliocentric chart help us establish Flow between the striving soul and the ever evolving Higher Self.

Even if we look at the Tropical chart as the personality level instead of life body level, the deeper karmic predisposition to our 'attitudes' and 'projects' comes from the soul level. They certainly then get played out in this life on the personality level. Remember Mary Burmeister gave us Jin Shin Jyutsu which works on the 3 levels of Physio-Philosophy, Physio-Psychology and Physio-Physiology. It takes the synching with Flow of all these levels to be fully functional Beings.

Steiner used examples which showed that the forces from the constellation stars were blocked or weakened by the planets in front of these constellations. He specifically compared the importance of these constellational stars to the rest of the stars as being of primary importance. This is why we quickly move past the Tropical level and move on to the Foundational Flows in this work as represented by the Sidereal zodiac of constellations.

This would be an appropriate place to remind ourselves that it is not the view that a planet 'out there' is 'doing something to us'. But according to the hermetic axiom, "As Above, So Below", there is a sympathetic and synchronistic relationship being mirrored in the gestural motif of meaning in the symbols involved.

"The birth chart is an image of the heavenly garment imprinted into and 'worn' by the human being from the moment of birth until the moment of death.

Foundational Flows

Contemplating images of the birth chart can inspire insights into how the human spirit's prenatal intentions are interwoven with the soul and living body throughout life and expressed in human biography.

The starry worlds we perceive with our senses are images of 'heaven' — the spiritual world we inhabit between death and rebirth. Zodiac, stars, and planets reflect working realms of spiritual beings that shape the human being — as physical body (form), etheric body (life), and astral body (consciousness). These spiritual beings fashioned the human vessel up to the stage at which the divine-human self-conscious 'I' (being) could be kindled on Earth…

Human beings develop the 'I' through perceiving, thinking, feeling, and acting creatively on Earth."

- Brian Gray – "Anthroposophic Foundations for a Renewal of Astrology"

Chapter 10
More on Thinking, Feeling and Willing at this Foundational Level

The subject of the 4-fold make-up of the human being – physical body, life body, soul and spirit bodies – will be deepened in another work I am presenting on the ego-organization and astrological symbology. It is also fully presented within the vast works of Rudolf Steiner which I humbly revere.

For our present purpose of dealing with the Foundational level work we will expand a little on why we are using Mercury, Venus and Mars as our birth chart representatives of Thinking, Feeling and Willing.

We will see some of the qualities associated with these planets so that these correlations at the Foundational level make sense. And here we will just point to the fact that other planets represent higher octaves of these same expressions. These other symbols and functions will then represent higher aspects of our soul and spirit as well. As was already stated these other levels are developed more fully elsewhere.

Let us start with some qualities of **Mercury - ☿**

The primary qualities of Mercury revolve around perception, processing of information on a mental level and communication. This translates to the soul level of consciousness we have been calling Thinking. Already it should be pointed out that there is an inherent flaw to this Mercury function right from the start. As Master Evolutionary Astrologer Steven Forrest points out, Mercury has its orbit so closely bound up with the Sun that it "literally orbits the ego".

https://www.forrestastrology.com/

Foundational Flows

And with this ego-conditioning, which comes with the gravity of the Sun's influence, there is also a karmic level emotional conditioning that is so well represented in the Moon symbolism. This primary function of perception, and the thinking that arises from it, is a potent reason we can use the Mercury placement as an indicator of the 'projects' that we come in with on the Thinking level of consciousness.

By 'project' then, we mean those colored and biased aspects of ourselves that hide in the shadows of our consciousness. They arise from the karmic conditioning that needs to be harmonized and cleared up so that we may continue to evolve as spiritual beings.

These 'projects' will be reflected throughout our entire being and are mirrored back to us from the outer world accordingly. This mirroring occurs due to the karmic bias in our perception that colors our experience. This then determines how we 'see' the world, and thus what we 'see' is our bias or 'project' being mirrored back to us. This is why we don't have pure and objective perception through any of our senses.

This is also why we can use the associated organ flow patterns of Jin Shin Jyutsu to assist in this process of re-harmonizing flow. They provide us with a hands-on method to bring Macrocosmic awareness and Flow into the Microcosmic body and soul prejudices. This level of Flow facilitates the openness needed to overcome rigid judgment coming from this karmically conditioned ego-coloring. The planetary positions give us precise and accurate information as to what and how change has to happen.

Venus - ♀

We are associating Venus at this Foundational level with the Feeling aspect of soul level consciousness. The Moon certainly is associated with the nervous system and the karmically conditioned emotional memory, but the soul or astral body level functioning of this consciousness is associated more with Venus.

Foundational Flows

Venus functions manifest as what Steiner refers to as Sympathy and Antipathy. This is the function that attracts or repels us to or away from objects on a felt sense level both externally and internally. It is an automatic function that arises prior to any thoughts that we then associate with it.

Venus is associated with the ability to build bridges with others in relationship. It also has to do with the ability of the emotional body to recuperate and heal after traumatic wounding. Here again we can use the astrological placement of Venus to find the appropriate organ flow pattern to use for the associated 'project'.

In the soul exercises that Rudolf Steiner gives, feeling is used to turbo-charge the effect when combining with thinking and willing.

Mars - ♂

Mars has the quality of being energetic, vitally alive and assertive. It is here associated with the soul level of consciousness associated with Willing.

Steven Forrest made a brilliant analogy of these 3 functions of Mercury, Venus and Mars with the 'Three Poisons' in Buddhism. The root poison is Ignorance, a Mercury, Thinking level functioning in discordance. Venus dysfunction becomes manifest as Desire. Mars function then manifests as the energy to acquire or protect, hold onto, or destroy and escape the object of sympathy or antipathy.

The soul body in its entirety as functioning consciousness is referred to by Steiner as our 'Desire body'. You can see how it can function in disharmony as our 'projects'. But in a healthy flowing way, it can furnish the evolutionary antidote. He also described our current level of awareness at a soul level as it regards these 3 functions with the following analogy.

"In the present stage of its evolution the human consciousness unfolds three forms, the waking, the dreaming, and the dreamless sleeping consciousness.

The waking consciousness experiences the outer world through the senses, forms ideas about it, and out of those ideas can create... The dreaming consciousness develops pictures in which the outer world is transformed… or his own inner world may appear before him in symbolic pictures… However, it is not possible to penetrate… these with understanding …because they are just too dim to rise into the waking consciousness and because what little may be perceived cannot be really understood…

In the dreamless sleep consciousness the soul passes through experiences which mean nothing more for the memory than an indifferent period of time between falling asleep and waking.

These experiences may be spoken of as non-existent, until the way into them has been opened up through spiritual scientific investigation."

– RS - Anthroposophical Leading Thoughts

https://wn.rsarchive.org/Books/GA026/English/RSP1973/GA026_a01.html

We can then make the following correlations as far as levels of conscious awareness –

Thinking	analogous to	Waking consciousness
Feeling	analogous to	Dream consciousness
Willing	analogous to	Dreamless sleep/unconsciousness

By doing the soul spirit work, for example, using the meditative exercises given by Rudolf Steiner, we can eventually transform these into levels of a more aware consciousness. Steiner names them as follows –

Thinking	transforms into	Imagination (Picture consciousness)
Feeling	transforms into	Inspiration (Feeling consciousness)
Willing	transforms into	Intuition (Consciousness in our Willing)

These transformed qualities are such that they may take lifetimes of work to accomplish. Only the highest initiates have done so in our time. But it is the work of our evolving consciousness. Rudolf Steiner tells us that specifically the work on the planet right now is the work on our soul, of transforming our body of desires.

This begins with the work of transforming our current brain-bound, reflective, sensory-based thinking into Imaginative consciousness. This has to be conscious soul work, there are no shortcuts. Steiner gives soul exercises using combinations of the 3 soul functions of Thinking, Feeling and Willing to do this work in a way that is appropriate and safe for our modern consciousness.

By only using these Foundational Flows as described in this book, it is no substitute for this conscious and vigorous soul work that it takes to evolve. But it will assist with Flow in a way that supports the awakening to the 'projects' we came in to work on that may have hindered us in this work for lifetimes. So combining the Foundational Flows with the appropriate soul work can be even more beneficial.

Another example of appropriate soul work in this regard is the Buddha's 8-Fold Path.

This is a path of compassionate awareness in developing the appropriate soul qualities within our consciousness. It is one of many possible pathways for the appropriate conscious soul work that an individual may choose for their personal path of spiritual development. The Foundational Flows are developed to provide individualized assistance along anyone's chosen path.

See Appendix for more on related soul/spiritual pathways.

Chapter 11
Rudolf Steiner and Christian Rosenkreutz

Rudolf Steiner developed 'Spiritual Science' which is called Anthroposophy. This he defined as follows -

"Anthroposophy is a path of cognition, to guide the Spiritual in the human being to the Spiritual in the universe. It arises in us as a need of the heart, of the life of feeling; and it can be justified only inasmuch as it can satisfy this inner need." - "Anthroposophical Leading Thoughts"

https://wn.rsarchive.org/Books/GA026/English/RSP1973/GA026_a01.html

This path is a fusion of the modern Rosicrucian path with the path of Esoteric Christianity. This path has everything to do with the alchemical marriage of soul and spirit. The symbols for this fusion include the Holy Grail and the Rose Cross.

The Rosicrucian path spoken of here is the revived path of Christian Rosenkreutz. It was Christian Rosenkreutz who was Steiner's main Master Teacher. The Rosicrucian path is based upon the initiation story of Christian Rosenkreutz in "The Chymical Wedding of Christian Rosenkreutz Anno 1459" by Johann Valentin Andreae.

"The Rosicrucian method of initiation is especially appropriate for today's humanity. It meets the needs of modern conditions. Not only is it a Christian path, but it enables those who strive to recognize that spiritual research and its achievements harmonize completely with modern culture and with the whole outlook of human beings today. For many centuries to come, Rosicrucianism will be the right method of initiation into spiritual life…

Unless one grasps what it means to overcome the lower, narrow self and what it means to rise to the higher self, it is impossible to understand the Cross as symbol of dying and becoming — the wood as the withering of lower self and the flowering roses as the becoming of higher self. Nor can we understand the words with which we shall close our discussion of Rosicrucianism. These words were also said by Goethe, and as a watchword they belong above the Cross wreathed in Seven Roses, symbolizing the sevenfold human being:

    Those who overcome themselves are free
    of the force that binds all humankind…

We are born out of the macrocosm. We must rediscover its forces and laws within ourselves as microcosms."
Rudolf Steiner – Berlin, March 14, 1907

https://wn.rsarchive.org/Lectures/GA055/English/AP1987/19070314p01.html

The Rose Cross meditation is powerfully described in Steiner's "Occult Science, An Outline". I would recommend looking this up as another powerful tool that could be used with your Foundational Flows.

What finally woke me up to using the birth chart to find the flows that we use as Foundational Flows comes from the following -

In Christopher Bamford's introduction to "The Secret Stream", a collection of Steiner's lectures on Rosicrucianism, he says that the Greeks were the first to add the rose to the cross. Plato talks of the World Soul crucified on the cross of the world.

"As for the rose, the Greeks derived it from rhodein, to flow… The Greeks then knew both the cross of the world, and the rose leading out of it. However, they only intuited the possibility of saving, that is, transforming, the world by uniting the Cross and the Rose. They did not yet possess the possibility of doing so. They already knew the union could exist, however, and even sought to bring the two — knowledge and love — together…"

Foundational Flows

It was seeing the Greek word for Flow used in this context that made a light go on for me. I had always been deeply impressed with Mary Burmeister's Jin Shin Jyutsu emphasis on 'Flow'. She described Flow as the essence of harmony at all levels of our 'Being'. Seeing 'Flow' used in the context of the Alchemical wedding and Rosicrucianism opened my eyes to the possibility of helping synchronize Flow between soul and the Higher Self in the ways we are describing with our Fundamental Flows.

Let me here emphasize again, our evolutionary growth depends on vigorous and conscious inner soul work. There are no short cuts.

The Foundational Flows described in this book are a way to harmoniously synch flow between our soul and Higher Self. This alone can bring a sense of calm and peaceful stress relief. One can be completely satisfied with that level of usage. But by increasing flow, as described, it may also more easily open up our awareness to the possible benefits of this conscious inner soul work. In this way we may find doorways opening spontaneously to help remind us of our path in a more conscious way. But these Foundational Flows will no doubt facilitate and enhance any soul/spiritual work that we choose to do in an ever increasingly conscious way.

Chapter 12
Depths with Fingers –

Learning about what is behind the gift of Self-Help in Jin Shin Jyutsu.

This figure shows the organ function level associations with the fingers –

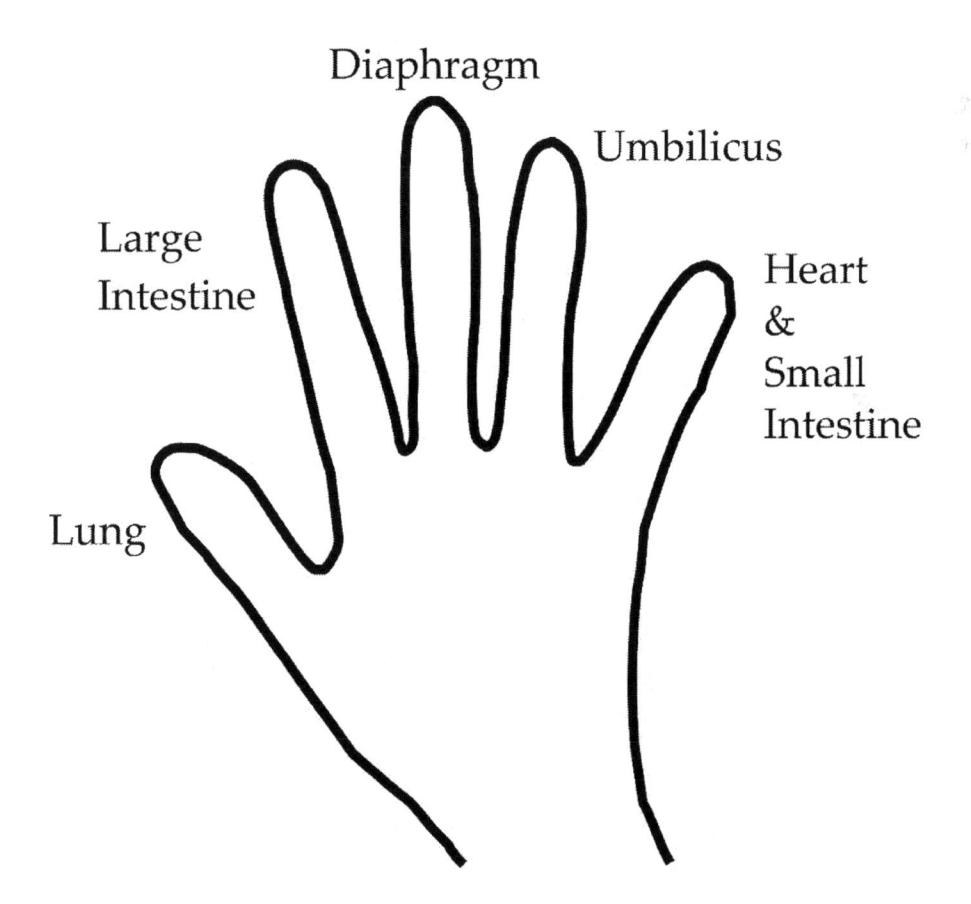

- Diaphragm
- Umbilicus
- Large Intestine
- Heart & Small Intestine
- Lung

Organ Function Level Finger Associations

Foundational Flows

The organ function level finger association is different from the Depth level finger associations. We can take advantage of these relationships when using the fingers for Self-Help when using our Foundational Flows in finger sequences. This way the individual can do the Self-Help finger sequences that correspond with their Foundational Flows anywhere and anytime, on their own. This can be in lieu of, or in addition to, receiving the Foundational Flows from other Jin Shin Jyutsu practitioners.

I point this out here because when we see the Foundational Flows used as Self-Help finger sequences we will notice that the fingers are used with their corresponding Depth level organ associations. There is one difference and that has to do with the 6th Depth Diaphragm and Umbilicus. Since there is no Depth level 'finger' for 6th Depth (it is associated with palm center) we use the Organ Function level associated finger (ring finger/Diaphragm – middle finger/Umbilicus) plus putting the thumb from the hand holding that finger into the palm center along with holding the finger. This helps bridge that 6th Depth level connection. For example –

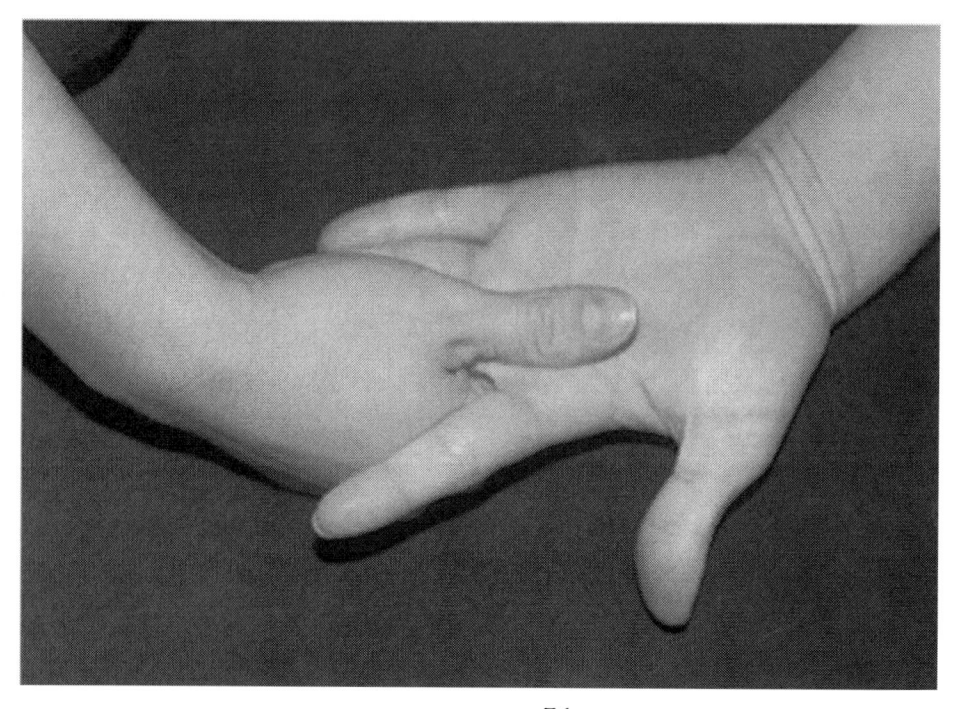

Foundational Flows

In this way we take advantage of both organ level and Depth level finger associations when using the 6th depth Diaphragm and Umbilicus.

We will now show the Depth level finger associations and then illustrate how to hold them for Self-Help in general as well as when we use them as Self-Help with our Foundational Flows.

This image gives us the Depth relationships with the fingers –

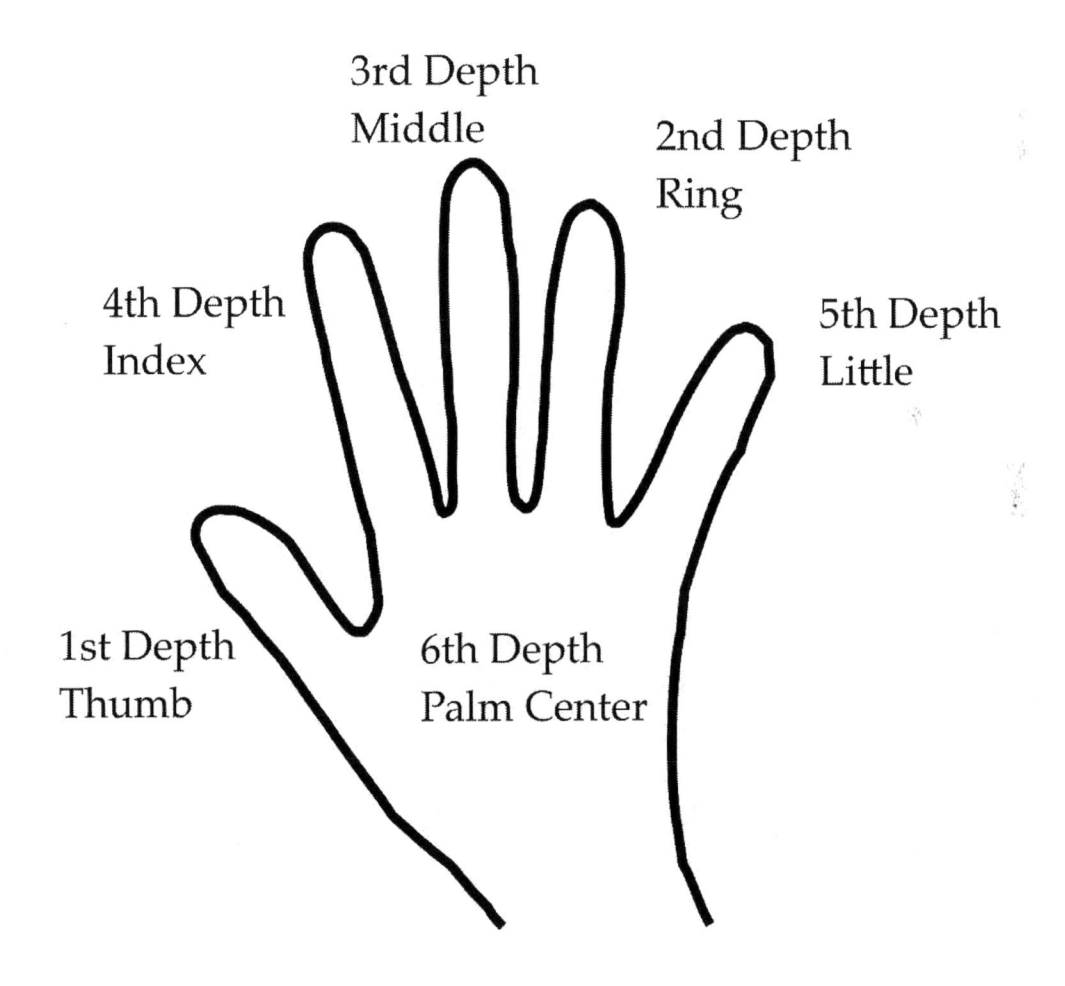

3rd Depth
Middle

2nd Depth
Ring

4th Depth
Index

5th Depth
Little

1st Depth
Thumb

6th Depth
Palm Center

Foundational Flows

We need to remember that the Depths correlate to the Elements or Phases in Traditional Chinese Medicine. These Finger associations are different than the organ relations which have to do with the meridian flows going through each finger which we showed first.

Now we see the Elemental relationships with the Depths and Fingers-

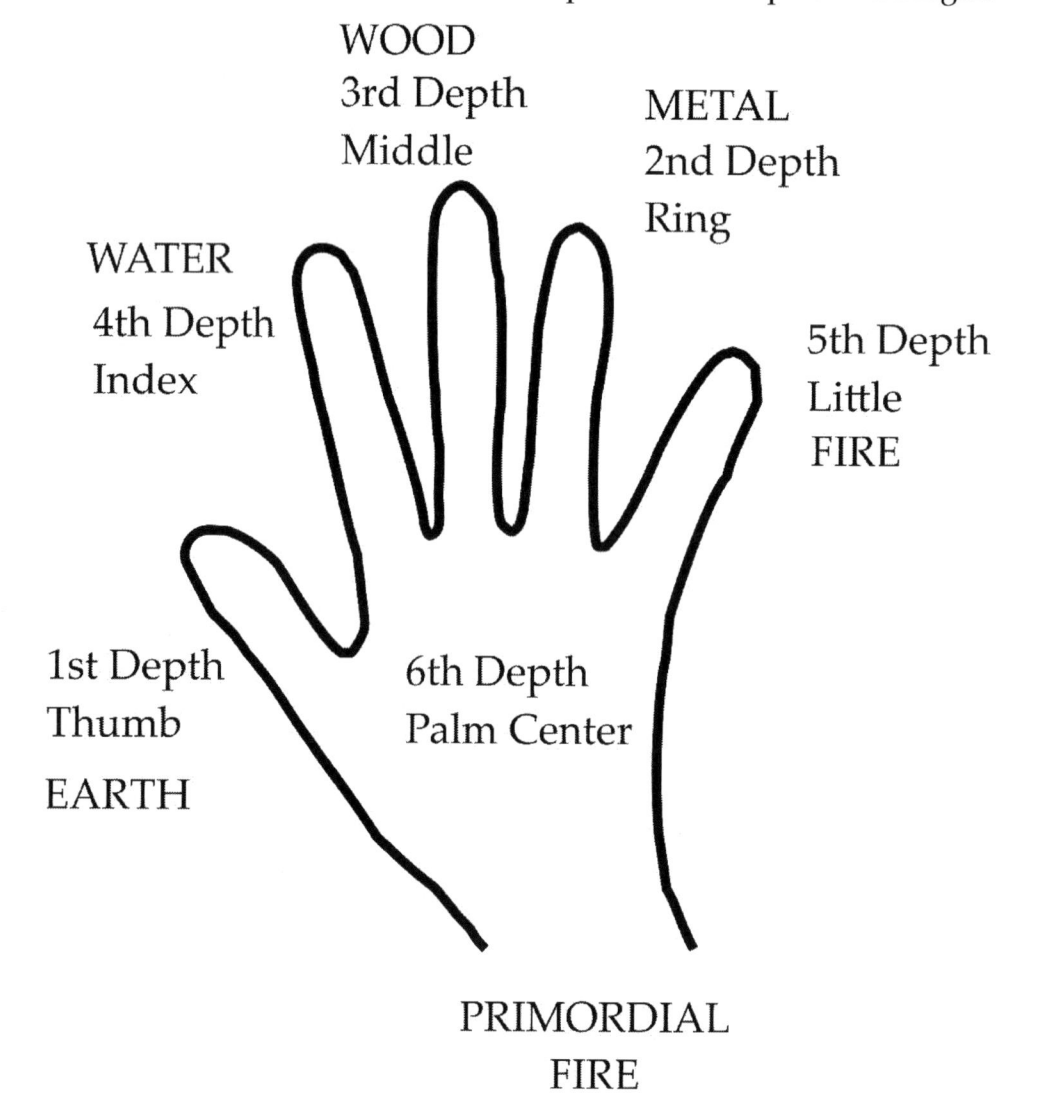

WOOD
3rd Depth
Middle

METAL
2nd Depth
Ring

WATER
4th Depth
Index

5th Depth
Little
FIRE

1st Depth
Thumb
EARTH

6th Depth
Palm Center

PRIMORDIAL
FIRE

Foundational Flows

In Jin Shin Jyutsu there is a slight difference in naming the elements from Traditional Chinese Medicine. In JSJ the term 'Air' is used where TCM uses 'Metal'. In this work I have used Metal in my diagrams, more as a carryback to my habit of thinking often as an acupuncturist than for any other reason.

Air is also a more traditional term used in the west, for example, the Greeks talked about Earth, Water, Fire, Air and Ether. The term Ether may actually match well with Wood due to its many associations with the Etheric or Life body. Mary Burmeister often used the term 'key' energy for Wood, referencing its important relationship to Ki or Qi movement.

Here we add the Organs associated with the (Elemental or) Depth level organ associations with the fingers –

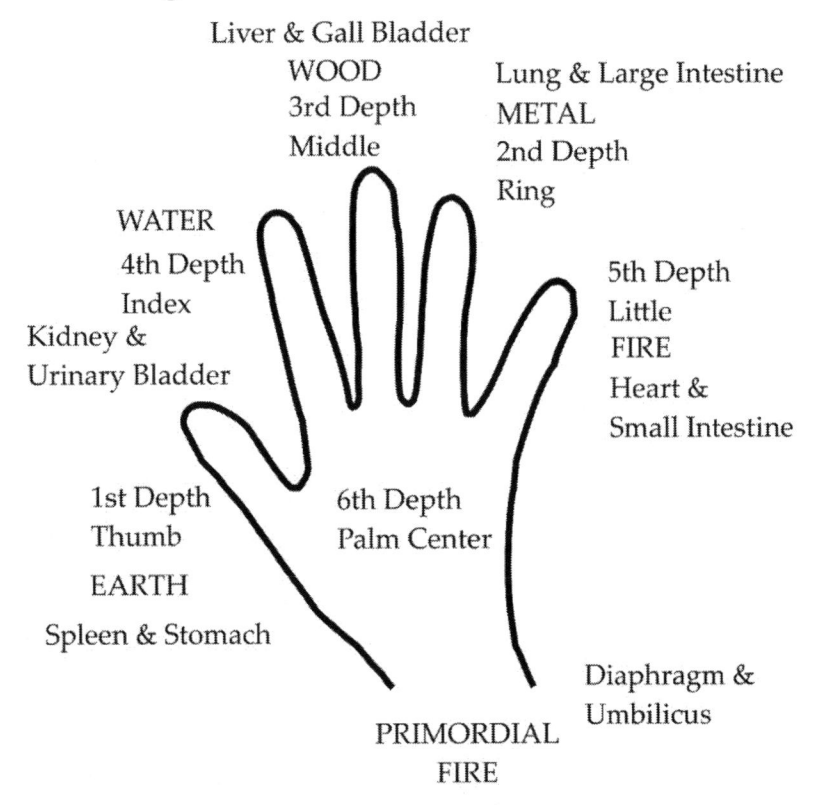

```
                    Liver & Gall Bladder
                    WOOD              Lung & Large Intestine
                    3rd Depth         METAL
                    Middle            2nd Depth
                                      Ring
        WATER
        4th Depth                              5th Depth
        Index                                  Little
    Kidney &                                   FIRE
    Urinary Bladder                            Heart &
                                               Small Intestine

        1st Depth      6th Depth
        Thumb          Palm Center
        EARTH
        Spleen & Stomach
                                          Diaphragm &
                                          Umbilicus
                       PRIMORDIAL
                       FIRE
```

Depth Level Finger Organ Associations

Chapter 13
Bringing in 'Self-Help' based on the Foundational Flows Individualized Finger Sequences and Mudras

Earlier we derived the following table as an example for using our Foundational Flows – we will now derive the Self-Help finger sequence which will be individualized for this person as well as the corresponding finger mudras –

Right side of body	*Left side of body*
Chart B – Soul Level	Chart C – Higher Self
Sidereal Geocentric Flows	Sidereal Heliocentric Flows
1) Willing Level — Mars (♂)	
Scorpio (♏) — Kidney	Libra (♎) — Urinary Bladder
2) Feeling Level — Venus (♀)	
Aquarius (♒) — Gall Bladder	Aries (♈) — Lung
3) Thinking Level — Mercury (☿)	
Capricorn (♑) — Umbilicus	Leo (♌) — Heart

Using the information from our last chapter we can now show the fingers associated with these Foundational Flows –

Foundational Flows

Right side of body	*Left side of body*
Chart B – Soul Level	Chart C – Higher Self
Sidereal Geocentric Flows	Sidereal Heliocentric Flows

1) Willing Level — Mars (♂)

Scorpio (♏) — Kidney Flow	Libra (♎) — Urinary Bladder Flow
Index Finger	Index Finger

2) Feeling Level — Venus (♀)

Aquarius (♒) — Gall Bladder Flow	Aries (♈) — Lung flow
Middle Finger	Ring Finger

3) Thinking Level — Mercury (☿)

Capricorn (♑) — Umbilicus Flow	Leo (♌) — Heart Flow
Ring Finger with Thumb in Palm	Little Finger

Now see the corresponding Foundational Flows Finger Sequence by itself –

Right Hand	Left Hand
Index Finger	Index Finger
Middle Finger	Ring Finger
Ring Finger with Thumb in Palm	Little Finger

Keep in mind that when it says Ring or Middle Finger with Thumb in the Palm center it is because Diaphragm and Umbilicus are 6th Depth. When we use the fingers for 6th Depth we connect the thumb of the hand holding the finger into the Palm center of the hand of that finger. This is because the Palm center is also a 6th Depth connection. This helps emphasize the 6th Depth connection with the Ring finger for Umbilicus (which would also be for either Lung or Large Intestine on a

Foundational Flows

Depth level associated with 2nd Depth). And it is the same with Diaphragm and the middle finger (which also has the 3rd Depth Liver and Gall Bladder association).

To clarify a little more, Middle finger has Diaphragm associated on an organ level and Liver and Gall Bladder on a Depth level. The Ring finger has Umbilicus associated on an organ level and Lung and Large Intestine on a Depth level. There is no Finger associated with the 6th Depth so we strengthen the connection if we are using the Middle or Ring finger for the 6th Depth organ level association by connecting it to the Palm center (bringing in 6th Depth) with the Thumb of the hand holding the finger. The Palm center is where the 6th Depth has its association on the hand at a Depth level.

This is therefore a way to take advantage of using the fingers for Self-Help specifically when we are using our individualized Foundational Flows.

Let us try and further clarify the finger Self-Help 'sequence' used in the previous examples, combining Chart B (Right hand) and Chart C (Left hand) associations –

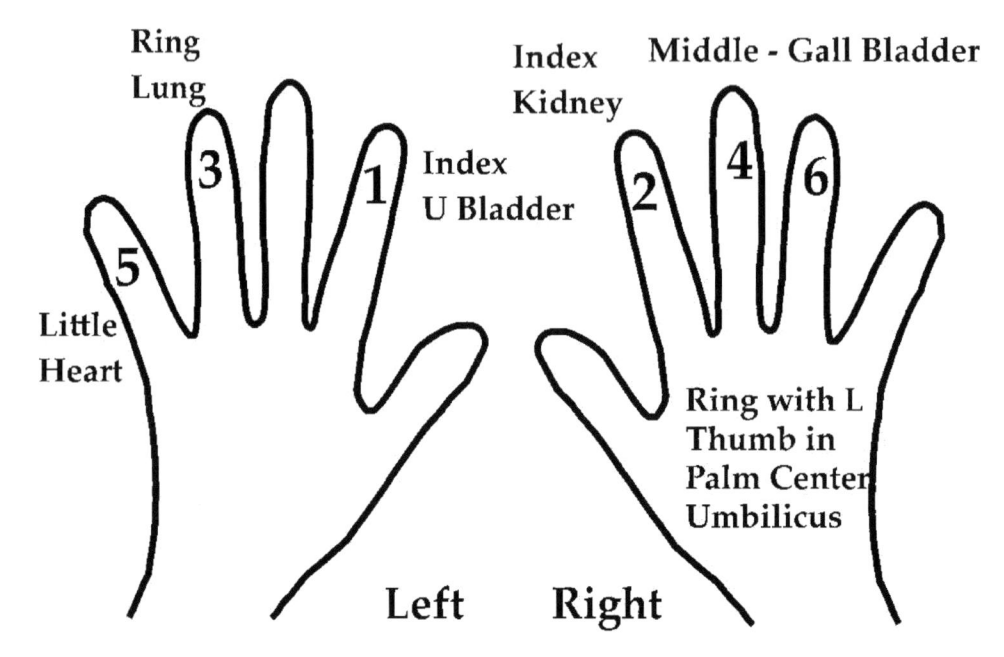

Ring
Lung

Index
Kidney

Middle - Gall Bladder

3   1   Index
U Bladder

2   4   6

5

Little
Heart

Ring with L
Thumb in
Palm Center
Umbilicus

Left   Right

Foundational Flows

The previous image shows the Foundational Flow Finger Self Help sequence for the example natal charts that we have been using. It shows the sequential steps by numbering the fingers and organs involved in the order they are to be held. If choosing to do this we hold each finger, in order, with 6 conscious and aware exhales and inhales.

This gives us a total of 6 finger holds with 6 breaths at each position which then gives us a total of 36 conscious and aware exhales and inhales. Mary Burmeister emphasized these 36 breaths as a powerful number of harmony and completion. After completing the sequence of holds with the 36 breaths I encourage you to hold your hands together in the following mudra with relaxed natural breathing until feeling centered and ready to move on into your day.

This final finger mudra is with fingers clasped and middle fingers extended together and palm centers together. This mudra is for connecting the whole body in functional flow with emphasis on the Main Central Universal Harmonizing Energy Flow.

Now let's look at examples of using this numbered finger sequence derived from this person's individualized Foundational Flows.

Foundational Flows

Foundational Flow Finger Sequence for Self-Help - Hold #1 – Left Index Finger from our example –

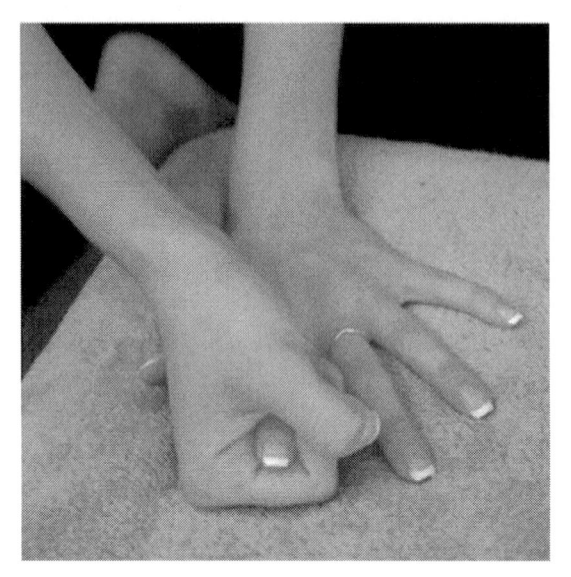

Foundational Flow Finger Sequence for Self-Help - Hold #2 – Right Index Finger from our example –

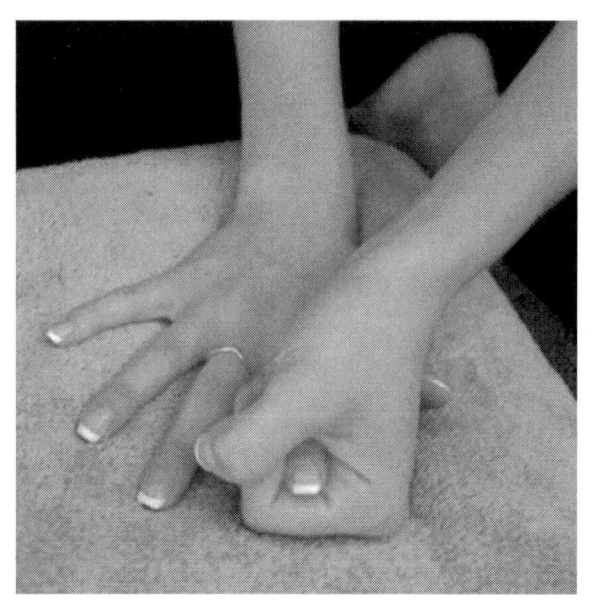

Foundational Flows

Foundational Flow Finger Sequence for Self-Help - Hold #3 – Left Ring Finger from our example –

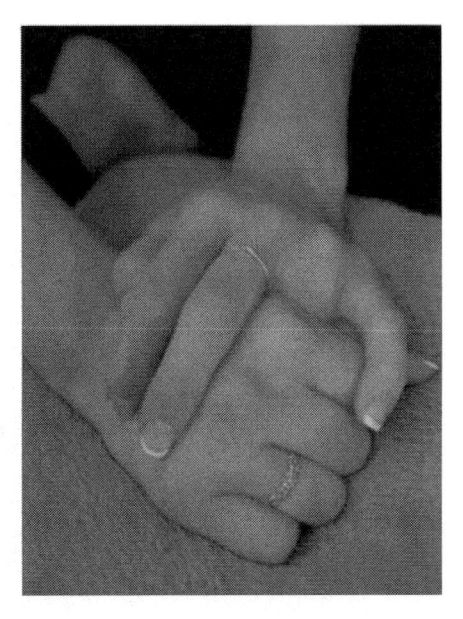

Foundational Flow Finger Sequence for Self-Help - Hold #4 – Right Middle Finger from our example –

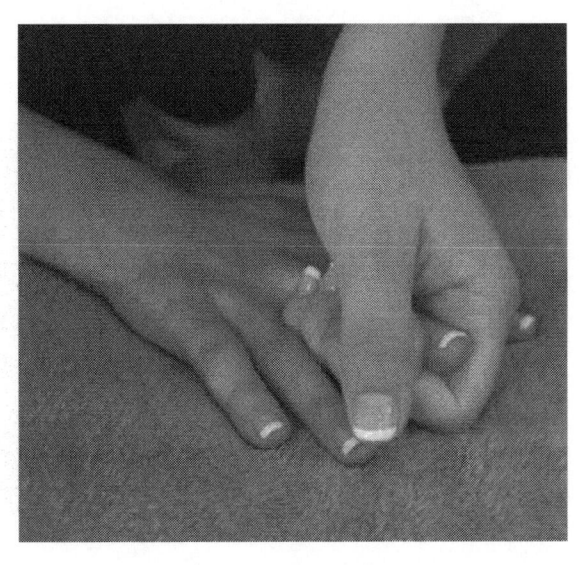

Foundational Flows

Foundational Flow Finger Sequence for Self-Help - Hold #5 – Left Little Finger from our example –

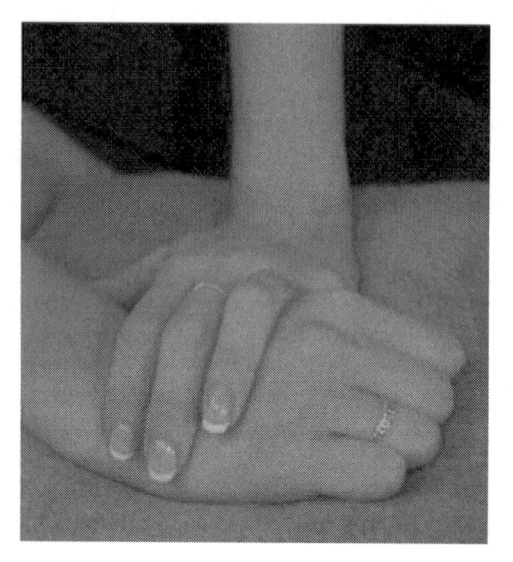

Foundational Flow Finger Sequence for Self-Help - Hold #6 – Right Ring Finger with thumb in palm center from our example –

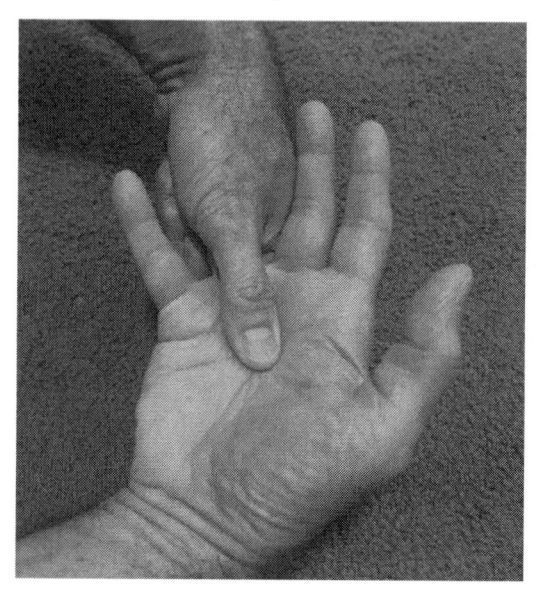

Foundational Flows

So if we review, we see that harmonizing flow between soul and spirit involves doing 6 organ flow patterns as two-sided trinities, simultaneously on the right and left sides of the body.

We can also take advantage of the finger Self-Help associations to these Foundational Flows to help ourselves. We do this in a sequential manner working through the six fingers alternating the hands with their corresponding trinities.

This means that the trinities are done on each hand just like the organ flow patterns are done on each side of the body. We just alternate side to side through the sequence if we are focusing on the 6 breaths per finger as described above. I do want to emphasize here that this is just one way to do this.

I strongly encourage individual creativity throughout this method, do what feels best. For example, if you have more time than 6 breaths each, spend more time with each finger. Focus more on feeling the pulse of energy in the fingers than on the number of breaths when you have more time. But it is still important to make full unforced conscious and aware exhales and inhales. The emphasis here is always on the exhale, if we completely let go, then the receiving of the abundance of the next breath naturally follows.

Here is another illustration of the relationships of the trinities and their numbered steps with the final mudra included in the middle. We are harmonizing soul and spirit using the soul qualities of consciousness – Thinking, Feeling and Willing. The upward pointing triangle represents the Higher Self Flows (Left side or hand) and downward pointing triangle has the Flows for soul (Right side or hand). The order of the numbers shows the sequence relative to the harmonizing of soul and Higher Self.

Foundational Flows

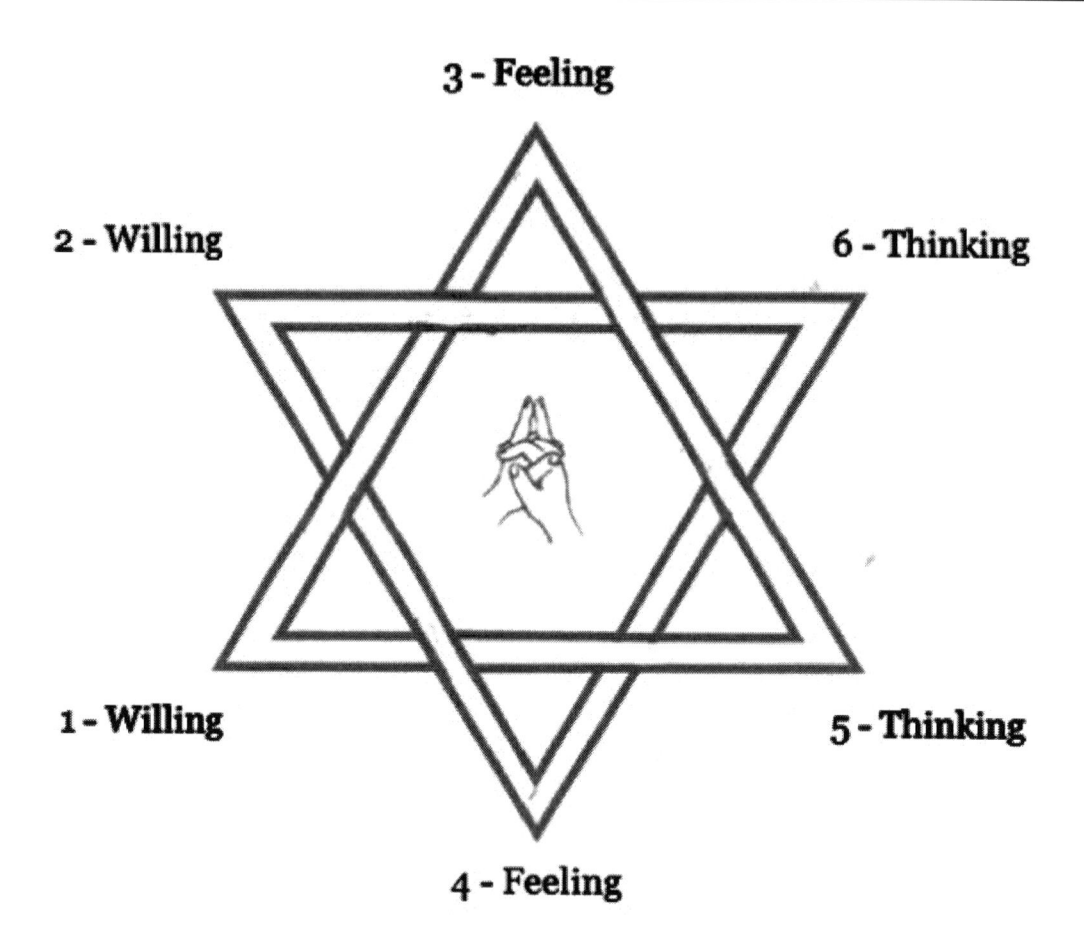

```
            3 - Feeling

2 - Willing              6 - Thinking



1 - Willing              5 - Thinking

            4 - Feeling
```

In Chapter 15 I will show a way of doing the trinities of right and left hands simultaneously using finger 'mudras' for the Foundational Flow positions as Self-Help. I will also mention how I came to the ordering of these sequences.

Chapter 14
Other relationship qualities of exploration

**Sayings for the signs - Organ qualities - Numbers
Flow - Essence/Project/Virtues**

First and foremost we are spiritual beings. We are woven together with the fabric of the cosmos all the way down into our physical body. We have a life body, a soul body and a spiritual nature permeating this entirely. Primeval Wisdom has described these interconnections within all traditions in slightly different ways. Today scientific thinking has narrowed down the focus to only the sense-perceptible aspect of our nature. This leaves out of consideration the greater vastness of who we are. Studying this enfolded fullness from these varied perspectives gives us many further ways to pursue the age-old dictum to "Know Thyself!"

We can point at a few more of these weaves that can further help ourselves and those we are working with to harmonize in flow right down into the physiology and its physical expression. Remembering the importance Steiner gave to consciousness as the disease vector we can pursue the interconnections and influence this has at all levels of our being.

This can only be a small introduction to these various ways of conscious exploration. Let creativity and intuition lead the way into the unexplored territory of our full expression.

Let us remember the interconnections between the astrological signs and the organ flow patterns of Jin Shin Jyutsu –

Foundational Flows

We can then add a list of energetic 'sayings' with the signs that give further insights into the gestural motif of those organ flow patterns – mentally, emotionally and physiologically.

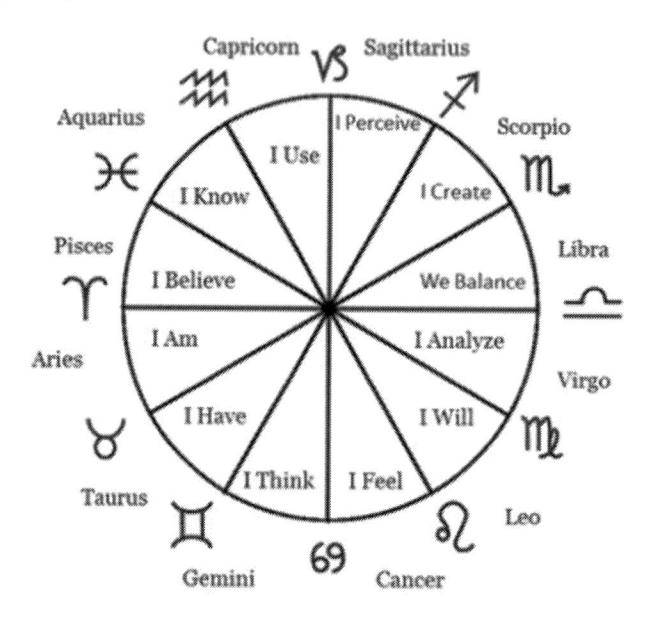

Foundational Flows

From the Foundational Flows examples we explored earlier, let's use the example of Mercury in Capricorn in the Geocentric Sidereal, or soul level chart, to explore ways to use this information–

Mercury (☿) Thinking – Capricorn (♑) Umbilicus

Capricorn says 'I Use'. With the Umbilicus function energy the specific question is 'How do I use the gifts I have been given?'

Umbilicus in TCM is the yang organ called Triple Burner, or San Jiao. In JSJ it is a 6th Depth organ which is an organ of Primordial Fire. It has more to do with our connection to our energetic blueprint as an avenue of Original Qi. It is said to have a name but no form, as a collection of insubstantial functions in the transformation of Qi. It nourishes all organs, it warms relationships. As a physical body harmonizer it brings mental emotional balance.

One might think then that in a healthy expression that this Mercury function of Thinking would have a positive warming and flowing effect physically, physiologically and in one's outer expression through energetic relationships. But if the planetary position actually expresses a weakness in function as a 'project', we might expect to see a more introverted gesture of this as an expression of the weakened function. I might then be seen as hindered in my ability to use these gifts of my thinking in the ways expressed by a healthy Umbilicus function.

TCM (Traditional Chinese Medicine) recognizes that the yin organs have soul/spiritual qualities. These qualities are then unfolded in the various elemental associations manifesting throughout all the manifold layers of our being – mentally, emotionally and physiologically. Here is an extremely short list of associations –

Heart – Fire – 5th Depth - Shen/Spirit/Mind

Liver – Wood – 3rd Depth – Hun/Ethereal Soul

Lungs – Metal – 2nd Depth - Po/Corporeal Soul

Spleen – Earth – 1st Depth – Yi/ Thought/Intellect

Kidneys – Water – 4th Depth – Zhi/Will Power

Let us use another example from our natal chart comparisons. This time we see from the Heliocentric (Higher Self level) birth chart that Venus is in Aries.

Venus (♀) Feeling – Aries (♈) – Lung

In TCM the Lung connection to the Po (Corporeal soul) connects us strongly to the feelings we are not conscious of. It is not a very mental quality of recognition of these feelings. As we see its association with the most basic and unconscious primitive function of respiration, it is easy to see why this level of feeling is at such a limited level of our conscious awareness. It is our awareness of pain on a physical level. And it is expressed in crying and weeping when we feel sadness and grief.

The Aries association of 'I Am' completely captures this type of awareness. In this case it boils down to 'I Am' what I Feel. But I have to become conscious of what I am feeling to then really know what 'I Am'.

In our example we see a weakness in this Venus/feeling function at an Aries/lung function energy level. A lack of awareness on a feeling level is compounded here and will be exacerbated by a diminished attunement to the impact that the feelings have on the breathing function. By governing respiration the lungs also govern qi. Since all emotions and sensations have a corresponding qi movement associated with them it will be extra important to strengthen this breathing function of the lungs to assist in the flow of qi and smoothing out the emotional level which is so unconscious here. Consciously working with the

Foundational Flows

breath will also be profoundly helpful here, especially in helping harmonize what it is this person is actually feeling.

This is why Mary Burmeister was so fond of saying "BE the Breath I am", capitalizing BE to put the emphasis on Breath Essence.

Another interesting way to explore the Foundational Flows and the meanings that they hold for us is to examine what Ageless Wisdom has to say about 'numbers.' There are qualitative essential meanings associated with numbers that go beyond the limiting quantitative values that we normally give them. In Jin Shin Jyutsu there are 26 Safety Energy Locks, each numbered 1 – 26, and each number has an 'essential meaning'. I here give an example from our previous Foundational Flows. And in Appendix 3 I will give a short list of the 1 – 26 numbered meanings.

In our example we had the Heliocentric Mercury (☿) in Leo (♌). Mercury is a thinking level soul quality here associated with the level of the Higher Self. This Mercury is blocking the constellation of stars known as Leo which is associated with Heart function energy. Therefore the function associated with thinking is weakened in "a heart way". The Heart is our place of deepest knowing. Perhaps this Mercury has difficulty getting quiet enough to calmly access this deep knowing.

Perhaps there is a constriction in the ability of this individual to connect with the spiritual intent of "bringing laughter into being" (Heart function energy). We could say joy is a quality that needs to be strengthened and this could be done by using the Foundational Flow indicated here, Heart functional energy organ flow pattern.

One way we can explore number in this situation is to look at the steps of the organ flow pattern itself. There are 7 steps to the flow pattern, 7 has the meaning of "Victory, Perfect life power". Since there are SEL's to be held at each of the 7 steps we can look at the qualitative meaning of the SEL at each step.

Foundational Flows

Heart Function Energy –

Left Flow – sitting on right side of body

Steps			Safety Energy Lock	
1st -	Head hand		left	11
	Foot hand		left	17
2nd -	Foot hand		right	22
3rd -	Foot hand		right	14
4th -	Foot hand		right	15
5th -	Foot hand		left	1
6th -	Foot hand		left	5
7th -	Foot hand		left	7

These are the steps for Heart function energy. For a chart diagram showing the positions of each SEL see –

https://www.jsjinc.net/proddetail.php?prod=SM-SELCHART

Foundational Flows

Let us look at the qualitative meanings of the SEL's being used in each step to try and discover another layer of meaning for the individual with this Foundational Flow.

1st step – SEL 11 – Justice, the hub, unload all 'excess baggage'

        SEL 17 – Relaxation of mind and nerves, reproductive energy

2nd step – SEL 22 – Complete, Gathering and Dispersal

3rd step – SEL 14 – Equilibrium, sustenance

4th step – SEL 15 – Joy and laughter, 'Wash our hearts with laughter'

5th step – SEL 1 – The prime mover, connecting the extreme height with the extreme depth

6th step – SEL 5 – Regeneration, putting off the old and putting on the new

7th step – SEL 7 – 'Victory', perfect life power

Meditating on the gestures of meaning behind each number can be insightful for seeing the antidotes to our 'projects'. We can build an imaginative story going through the numbers of the SEL's in each step. We can even point these out in a gentle way with our clients when doing these Foundational Flows with them. In this way we are more consciously engaging our core 'attitudes' and 'projects' we have to meet in order to make appropriate changes for growth.

Yet another way to explore the meaning behind the Foundational Flows is to dig deeper into the gesture of the Depths or Elemental Phases. These aspects have 3 main levels of expression. These 3 levels are known as the Essence level, the Attitude level and the Virtue level.

Foundational Flows

Here we have the finger associations with the depths –

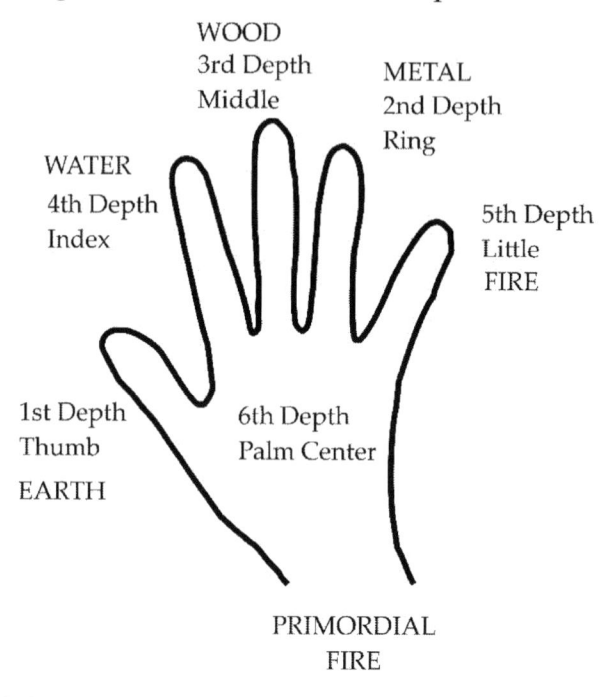

```
                WOOD
             3rd Depth      METAL
              Middle     2nd Depth
                            Ring
   WATER
  4th Depth
    Index                     5th Depth
                               Little
                                FIRE

  1st Depth   6th Depth
    Thumb    Palm Center
    EARTH

              PRIMORDIAL
                FIRE
```

This diagram will show us the Essence level Depth and Finger associations

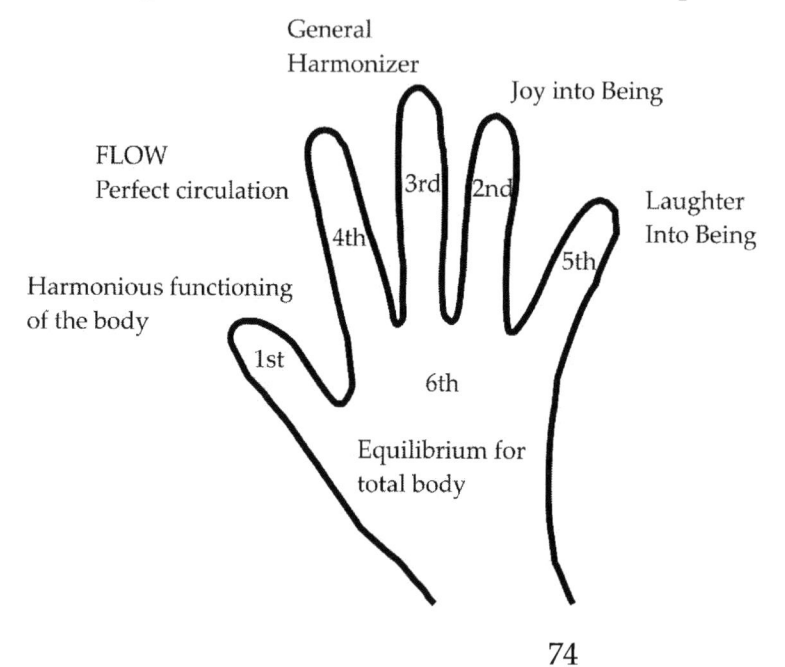

```
              General
             Harmonizer
                       Joy into Being
   FLOW
  Perfect circulation   3rd  2nd     Laughter
                    4th           Into Being
                              5th
  Harmonious functioning
  of the body
                1st
                       6th

              Equilibrium for
              total body
```

74

Foundational Flows

This diagram will show us the Attitude level Depth and Finger associations

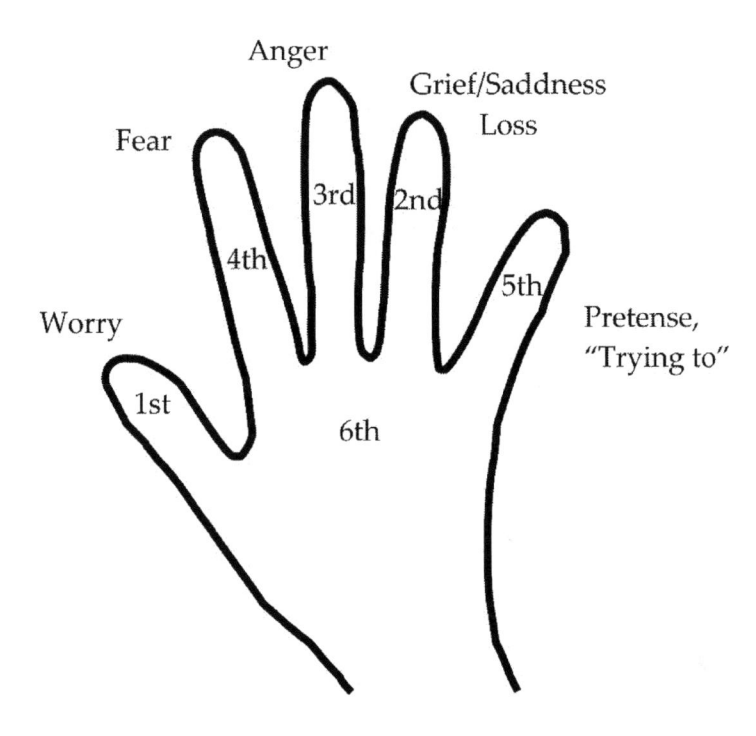

```
        Anger
              Grief/Saddness
  Fear          Loss
         3rd  2nd
       4th
              5th
  Worry          Pretense,
    1st          "Trying to"
          6th
```

The Attitude level is what we have made of our gifts (essence level) from Creator. The 'attitude' is an imperfect reflection, the karmic level 'project' we are working on in this life.

Foundational Flows

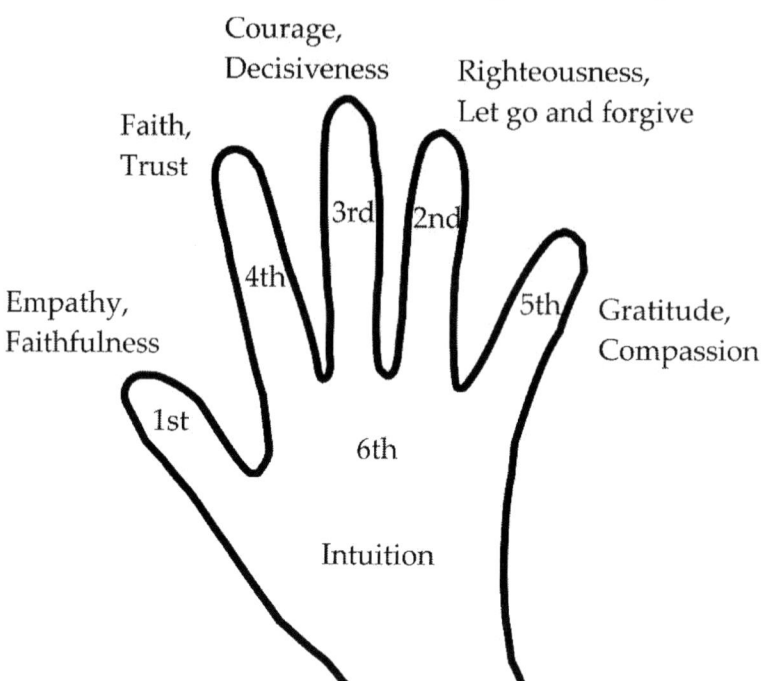

This next diagram shows us the Virtue level Depth and Finger associations

```
                    Courage,
                    Decisiveness    Righteousness,
        Faith,                      Let go and forgive
        Trust
                       3rd   2nd
                   4th
   Empathy,                      5th    Gratitude,
   Faithfulness                         Compassion
              1st
                        6th

                      Intuition
```

The Virtue level shows us the antidote, the soul level work, to consciously build the bridge to our Higher Self and reharmonize in Flow back to the essence level we were originally given. And then we Flow in a new conscious aware state of BEing.

Chapter 15
Foundational Flow Mudras and the Foundation Stone Meditation

When I started out with the Foundational Flows I always used my finger sequences in the order of Thinking, Feeling and then Willing. Along with this order I also went with soul first (Right hand and side) and then spirit (Left hand and side) with my finger sequences.

Then one day I had an epiphany. I was reading aloud Rudolf Steiner's Foundation Stone meditation and while I was doing this I was holding a finger mudra for my Foundational Flows. What I was holding wasn't necessarily a traditional finger mudra, but just a way of engaging the finger associated with my Foundational Flows. I was doing this with both hands simultaneously as I read the meditation.

The epiphany that I received was to do the Foundational Flows in the exact opposite order that I had always done. This means to go in the order of Willing, Feeling and then Thinking. But not only this, I now go in the order of spirit (Left hand and side) and then soul (Right hand and side). In other words, I am now doing my Self-Help finger sequences in the exact opposite order from how I started doing them.

In that moment I knew that this had an even deeper effect, truly more Foundational, than what I had been doing. I don't think that this meant that what I had done before was necessarily wrong. But I think that this new way is more essential. The way I had always done before was really just a habit based on hearing or seeing that the soul qualities Steiner describes were always stated as – Thinking, Feeling and Willing.

Using our example charts and their associated finger holds, and going through the Foundation Stone meditation, this is what we would have –

Foundational Flows

both willing fingers held together (as I will demonstrate) with the first section of the meditation, then both feeling level fingers with the second section, then both thinking level fingers with the third section and finally the final mudra with section 4.

You will see that in the Foundation Stone meditation, Steiner goes in the order of Willing, Feeling and then Thinking with a following 4th section. If we notice the web of manifestation that he weaves in at each level we get a hint at the grand complexity and beauty behind our BEing and the meditation itself. It is about becoming increasingly conscious of our spiritual inheritance. Below is a diagram showing some of the terms used in the meditation that might help us see into this complex weaving.

```
            Father
             /\
            /  \
           /    \
       Son ------ Holy Spirit
```

First Hierarchy	SERAPHIM CHERUBIM THRONES	Spirits of Love Spirits of Harmony Spirits of Will	
Second Hierarchy	DOMINIONS VIRTUES POWERS	Spirits of Wisdom Spirits of Motion Spirits of Form	Kyriotetes Dyamis Exusiai, Elochim
Third Hierarchy	ARCHAI ARCHANGELS ANGELS	Spirits of Personality Spirits of Fire Spirits of Twilight	First Beginnings Spirits of the Age Archangeloi Angeloi

MAN: The Hierarchy of Love and Freedom

Ephesians 1:21

Foundational Flows

This is section 1, to be held with the willing fingers while being read aloud.

The Foundation Stone Meditation

Human Soul!
You live in the limbs,
Which bear you through the world of space
Into the spirit's ocean-being:
Practice spirit-recalling
In depths of soul
Where in the wielding
World-Creator-Being
Your own I
Comes into being
Within the I of God;
And you will truly live
In human cosmic being.

For the Father-Spirit of the heights holds sway
In depth of worlds begetting life
Spirits of Strength:
Seraphim, Cherubim, Thrones,
Let from the heights ring forth
What in the depth finds its echo,
Speaking:
Ex Deo Nascimur,
Out of the Godhead we are born.

This is heard by the spirits of the elements
In East, West, North, South:
May human beings hear it!

Remember our example charts had the Willing fingers as follows – The left hand (Higher Self level) was Index finger (for Urinary Bladder). The right hand (soul level) was Index finger (for Kidney). It would look like the following, and both fingers would be held at the same time while part one of the meditation is read aloud.

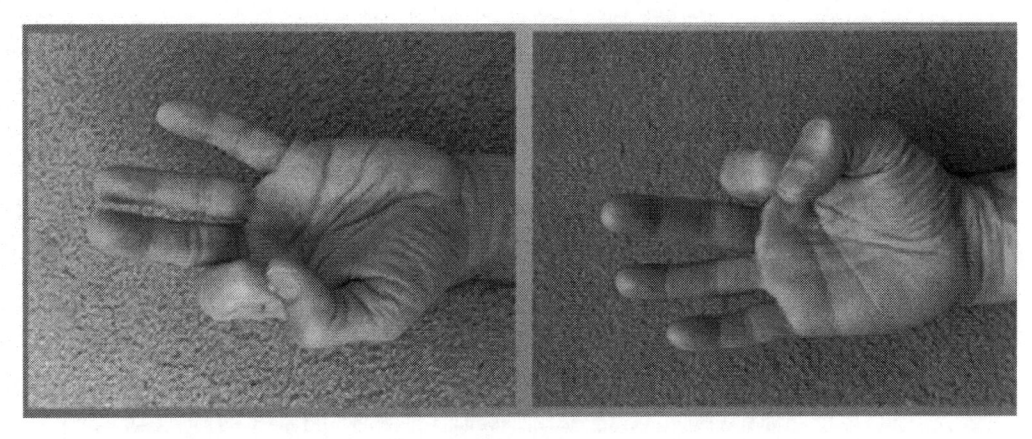

Foundational Flows

The Feeling fingers are held with the second section of the Foundation Stone Meditation.

Human soul!
You live within the beat of heart and lung
Which leads you through the rhythms of time
Into the feeling of your own soul-being
Practice spirit-sensing
In equanimity of soul,
Where by the surging
Deeds of world-becoming
Unite your own I
With the I of the World;
And you will truly feel
In human soul's creating.

For the Christ-will encircling us holds sway,
In world rhythms, bestowing grace upon souls.
Spirits of Light:
Kyriotetes, Dynamis, Exusiai,
Let from the East be enkindled
What through the West takes on form,
Speaking:
In Christo morimur
In Christ death become life.

This is heard by the spirits of the elements
In East, West, North, South:
May human beings hear it!

Remember our example charts had the Feeling fingers as follows – The left hand (Higher Self level) was Ring finger (for Lung). The right hand (soul level) was Middle finger (for Gall Bladder). It would look like the following, and both would be held at the same time while part two of the meditation would be read aloud.

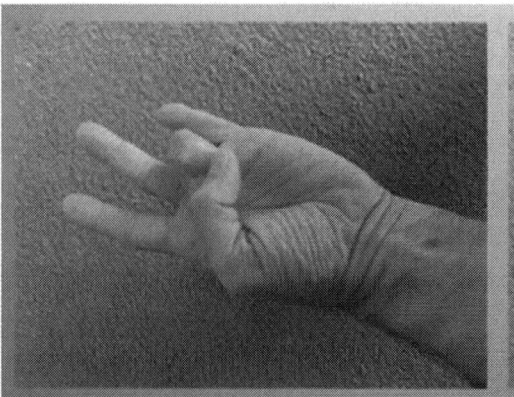

Foundational Flows

The Thinking fingers are held with the third section of the Foundation Stone Meditation.

Human soul!
You live within the resting head
Which from the ground of eternity
Unlocks for you world-thoughts:
Practice Spirit-beholding
In stillness of thought,
Where god's eternal aims
Bestow the light of cosmic being
On your own I
For free and active willing;
And you will truly think
In human spirit depths.

For the Spirits' world-thoughts hold sway
In cosmic being, imploring light.
Spirits of Soul,
Archai, Archangeloi, Angeloi,
Let from the depths be entreated
What in the heights will be heard,
Speaking:
Per Spiritum Sanctum reviviscimus
In the spirit's cosmic thoughts the soul awakens.

This is heard by the spirits of the elements
In East, West, North, South:
May human beings hear it!

Remember our example charts had the Thinking fingers as follows – The left hand (Higher Self level) was Little finger (for Heart). The right hand (soul level) was Ring finger (for Umbilicus). It would look like the following, and both would be held at the same time while part three of the meditation would be read aloud.

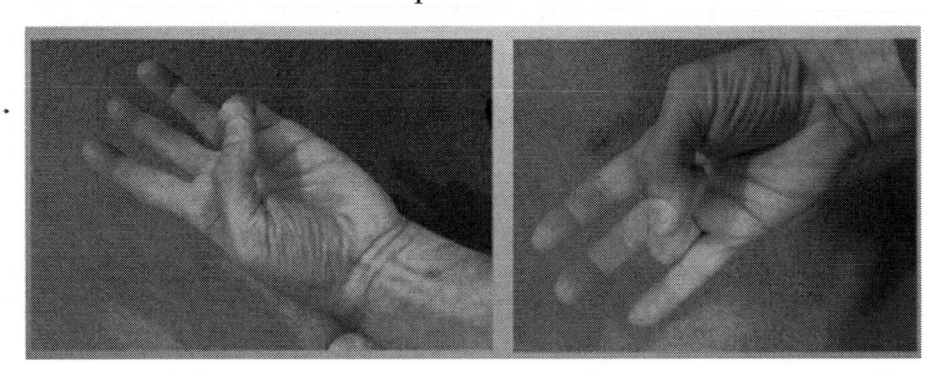

Foundational Flows

The 4th section of the Foundation Stone Meditation with the Final Finger Mudra

At the turning point of time	**Light divine;**
The Spirit-light of the world	**Christ-Sun**
Entered the stream of earth existence.	**Warm**
	Our hearts;
Darkness of night	**Enlighten**
Had ceased its reign;	**Our heads,**
Day-radiant light	**That good may become**
Shone forth in human souls;	**What from our hearts**
Light	**We are founding,**
That gives warmth	**What from our heads**
To simple shepherds' hearts;	**We direct,**
Light	**With focused will.**
That enlightens	
The wise heads of kings;	

Further clarifying, using the 4 sections of the meditation with the fingers – The meditation shows the macrocosmic enfolding of these spiritual forces into the microcosm. This is what we take advantage of using our Foundational Flows.

The Father-Spirit forces and 1st Hierarchy of Spirit beings are folded into their microcosmic reflection in the body and soul as the metabolic-limb forces. This is the Willing polarity.

The Son forces and 2nd Hierarchy of Spirit beings are folded into the middle region. This is the rhythmic system of Feeling in the soul, reflected in heart and lung.

The Spirit's world thoughts and 3rd Hierarchy of Spirit beings are folded into the upper polarity as Thinking in the resting head.

Foundational Flows

Thus the Trinity of the macrocosm is enfolded into all levels of our being as trinity even into the microcosm of the body and soul.

Using the Foundational Flows in the order here shown through the Foundation Stone Meditation makes sense on many levels. Steiner talked about accessing the will through the spirit by doing soul/spiritual work. He juxtaposed this against the improper way of trying to forcefully influence willing. He talked about this specifically in the lecture series "From Jesus to Christ". The Jesuits emphasized the Jesus-principle (earthly man), the Rosicrucians emphasized the Christ-principle (cosmic man) in the approach to the Will. Steiner revealed that the illegitimate approach to influencing the will is what leads to trying to enforce ones will over another.

By connecting to source (spirit) first, which is what is behind the willing function, we may properly bring thinking 'on-line' into a new level of awareness.

"The Rosicrucians have always wished to adhere strictly to the rule that even in the highest regions of Initiation nothing must be worked upon except the Spirit-element which, as common between man and man, is available in the evolution of humanity. The Initiation of the Rosicrucians was an Initiation of the Spirit. It was never an Initiation of the Will, for the Will of man was to be respected as a sanctuary in the innermost part of the soul. Hence the individual was led to those Initiations which were to take him beyond the stage of Imagination, Inspiration, and Intuition, but always so that he could recognize within himself the response which the development of the Spirit-element was to call forth. No influence was to be exerted on the Will.

We must not mistake this attitude for one of indifference towards the Will. The point is that by excluding all direct working upon the Will, the purest spiritual influence was imparted indirectly through the Spirit. When we come to an understanding with another man with regard to entering on the path of knowledge of the Spirit, light and warmth are radiated from the spiritual path, and they then enkindle the Will, but always by the indirect path through the Spirit — never otherwise...

Foundational Flows

In Rosicrucianism, therefore, we can observe in the highest sense that impulse of Christianity which finds twofold expression: on the one hand in the Son-element, in the Christ-working which goes down deeply into the subconscious; on the other, in the Spirit-working which embraces all that falls within the horizon of our consciousness. We must indeed bear the Christ in our Will; but the way in which men should come to an understanding with each other in life concerning the Christ can be found only — in the Rosicrucian sense — through a conscious soul-life which penetrates ever more deeply into our hidden nature.

In reaction against many other spiritual streams in Europe, the opposite way was taken by those who are usually called Jesuits. The radical, fundamental difference between what we justifiably call the Christian way of the Spirit and the *Jesuit* way of the Spirit, which gives a one-sided exaggeration to the Jesus-Principle, is that the intention of the *Jesuit* way is to work directly, at all times, upon the Will. The difference is clearly shown in the method by which the pupil of Jesuitism is educated. Jesuitism is not to be taken lightly, or merely exoterically, but also esoterically, for it is rooted in esotericism. It is not, however, rooted in the spiritual life that is poured out through the symbol of Pentecost, but it seeks to root itself directly in the Jesus-element of the Son, which means in the Will; and thereby it exaggerates the Jesus-element of the Will."

Rudolf Steiner – "From Jesus to Christ" – Chapter 1

https://wn.rsarchive.org/Lectures/GA131/English/RSP1973/19111005p02.html

We are taking advantage of the fact that we can hold both fingers at the same time by using them as a 'mudra'. The finger of focus is held with the nail of that finger under the Thumb pad as pictured. In this way we can use any finger combination.

Mary Burmeister gives a list of special finger mudras in her texts. These were the mudras that Jiro Murai used to heal himself. It was the start of his journey into re-discovering Jin Shin Jyutsu. These mudras are to be used with reverence and devotion.

Mary also gave lots of 'quickies' and Self-Help combinations which used 'mudras' more in line with what I have shown here with the Foundation Stone meditation. So I truly feel that this can be an appropriate way of engaging Flow by using the fingers in this way.

The more traditional way of using fingers in Self-Help has been shown – holding one finger at a time while emphasizing conscious exhaling and inhaling with an awareness of feeling the held finger pulse with energy. This shows the connection with Flow that is being engaged.

I find it especially useful if I am in an activity where it is not as easy to hold a finger with your other hand. For example, when I hike I often use the finger mudras as I have shown, with both hands simultaneously using my Foundational Flow finger sequence. I will do this as I have shown in the Foundation Stone meditation. I hold the two Willing fingers as a 'mudra' simultaneously first. Then hold the Feeling level and then the Thinking level.

Be creative in your use of these techniques. Individualize their usage to fit your lifestyle. The more we use them the more we engage Flow. Engaging Flow with consciousness, especially with our breath, has a powerful effect in building the bridge between soul and spirit.

Chapter 16
Closing the Foundation – Looking ahead

Combining the wisdom inherent in Jin Shin Jyutsu, Astrology and Anthroposophy provides us with a unique and individualized way of addressing the 'projects' and 'attitudes' we come into this life working on.

We have dipped our toes in the depth and unity of the Ageless Wisdom traditions. We have seen the value of a spiritual cosmology for answering the age-old call to 'Know Thyself!' And we can see that to truly know one's self involves an understanding of our 3-fold nature as it expresses itself in the 3 worlds – physical world, soul world and spiritual world. To neglect any one of these only furthers disharmony.

We have discovered a tool for working with the fullness of our Being in a simple yet powerful way. It is with the Foundational Flows that we can help others in very specific ways to connect and center themselves deeply within their spiritual center. Any individual can use the Self-Help finger sequences and mudras to do the same for themselves. Combining these Flows with conscious soul work can help us in building the bridge of re-connection to our spiritual nature and rediscover that true nature in a meaningful way.

From simply easing stress in our complicated lives to actively harmonizing soul and spirit, these individualized Foundational Flows are worth discovering and exploring in ever increasingly creative ways. I hope that you find this to be true for you.

You have learned in this manual how to find the positions in your astrological birth chart that are then used to determine your Foundational Flows.

You have learned how to find which organ flow patterns to use once these natal birth positions have been determined.

Foundational Flows

You have also seen the progression of my development of this technique and why I now use the order of Willing, Feeling and Thinking.

If you are a Jin Shin Jyutsu practitioner you can use these Foundational Flows with your clients and even deepen the relationship you have with them.

Any one of us can take advantage of the Foundational Flows by using the derived Self-Help finger sequences alone, without the help of another.

If you are also an astrologer you can use most available programs to help you find the information needed to proceed. You just need to use settings with the appropriate zodiacs to derive the charts. If you don't have this tool but want to have this information available for your personal use or to help with your clients, visit my website (https://erbdoc.com/flows) where you can enter your birth information and I can email your Foundational Flows and/or Self-Help finger sequences to you.

This is the Foundational Level Course and in time we will move on to further levels to continue to deepen our connection to 'Self'.

Appendix 1
Some paths emerging from the heart of Ageless Wisdom

6 Accessory Exercises

8-fold path of Buddha

Initiation prior to the Mystery of Golgotha

7 stages of the Rosicrucian Method

7 steps of Esoteric Christian path

Petalamund

In this appendix we will give a brief look at various paths connected to those we have used in this work on the Foundational Flows. These will be brought in here merely as hints of paths of further study for anyone wanting to deepen this soul/spiritual work. All will be worth the time spent pondering and meditating on. This appendix is by no means exhaustive.

The 'Six Accessory Exercises' – Rudolf Steiner

Rudolf Steiner emphasized that the exercises he gives here are safe and appropriate for our time. They are specific ways that he gives of combining Thinking, Feeling and Willing in a set of exercises to develop the soul/spiritual bridge and connection. Please go to the source to get the complete description.

"The **first condition** is the cultivation of absolutely clear thinking. For this purpose a man must rid himself of the will-o'-the-wisps of thought, even if only for a very short time during the day - about five minutes (the longer, the better). He must become the ruler in his world of thought. He is not the ruler if external circumstances... determine a thought and how he works it out.

When this exercise has been practiced for, say, one month, a **second** requirement should be added. We try to think of some action which in the ordinary course of life we should certainly not have performed. Then we make it a duty to perform this action at a fixed time every day...

In the **third** month, life should be centered on a new exercise - the development is on certain equanimity towards the fluctuations of joy and sorrow, pleasure and pain...

In the **fifth** month, efforts should be made to develop the feeling of confronting every new experience with complete open-mindedness...

In the **sixth** month, endeavors should be made to repeat all the five exercises again, systematically and in regular alternation. In this way a beautiful equilibrium of soul will gradually develop..."

From Rudolf Steiner – "Guidance in Esoteric Training"

https://wn.rsarchive.org/Lectures/GA245/English/GuidEsot05.html

Foundational Flows

The 'Eightfold Path' and Rudolf Steiner

"FOR THE DAYS OF THE WEEK

The pupil must pay careful attention to certain activities in the life of soul which in the ordinary way are carried on carelessly and inattentively. There are eight such activities. It is naturally best to undertake only one exercise at a time, throughout a week or a fortnight, for example, then the second, and so on, then beginning over again. Meanwhile it is best for the eighth exercise to be carried out every day. True self-knowledge is then gradually achieved and any progress made is perceived.

The Eight Exercises

1	Saturday	♄	Right Thinking
2	Sunday	☉	Right Resolves
3	Monday	☽	Right Speaking
4	Tuesday	♂	Right Action
5	Wednesday	☿	Right Way of Life
6	Thursday	♃	Right Endeavor
7	Friday	♀	Right Remembrance
8	Plus:		Right Meditation

Foundational Flows

SATURDAY

To pay attention to one's ideas. To think only significant thoughts. To learn little by little to separate in one's thoughts the essential from the nonessential, the eternal from the transitory, truth from mere opinion. In listening to the talk of one's fellow-men, to try and become quite still inwardly, foregoing all assent, and still more all unfavorable judgments (criticism, rejection), even in one's thoughts and feelings. This may be called: 'RIGHT OPINION'.

SUNDAY

All unthinking behavior, all meaningless actions, should be kept far away from the soul. One should always have well-weighed reasons for everything. And one should definitely abstain from doing anything for which there is no significant reason...This may be called: 'RIGHT JUDGMENT' having been formed independently of sympathies and antipathies.

MONDAY

Talking. Only what has sense and meaning should come from the lips of one striving for higher development. All talking for the sake of talking - to kill time - is in this sense harmful...This does not mean shutting oneself off from intercourse with one's fellows; it is precisely then that talk should gradually be led to significance...First listen quietly; then reflect on what has been said. This exercise may be called: `RIGHT WORD'.

TUESDAY

External actions...Where one does things of one's own accord, out of one's own initiative: consider most thoroughly beforehand the effect of one's actions. This is called: `RIGHT DEED'.

WEDNESDAY

The ordering of life. To live in accordance with Nature and Spirit. Not to be swamped by the external trivialities of life. To avoid all that brings unrest and haste into life. To hurry over nothing, but also not to be indolent...One speaks in this connection of 'RIGHT STANDPOINT'.

THURSDAY

Human Endeavor…To look beyond the everyday, the momentary, and to set oneself aims and ideals connected with the highest duties of a human being…This can be summed up as: 'TO LET ALL THE FOREGOING EXERCISES BECOME A HABIT'.

FRIDAY

The endeavor to learn as much as possible from life. Nothing goes by us without giving us a chance to gain experiences that are useful for life…One can learn from everyone - even from children if one is attentive. This exercise is called: 'RIGHT MEMORY'. (Remembering what has been learnt from experiences).

SUMMARY

To turn one's gaze inwards from time to time, even if only for five minutes daily at the same time. In so doing one should sink down into oneself, carefully take counsel with oneself, test and form one's principles of life, run through in thought one's knowledge - or lack of it - weigh up one's duties, think over the contents and true purpose of life, feel genuinely pained by one's own errors and imperfections…This exercise is called: 'RIGHT EXAMINATION'."

- From Rudolf Steiner – "Guidance in Esoteric Training"

https://wn.rsarchive.org/Lectures/GA245/English/GuidEsot05.html

Initiation prior to the Mystery of Golgotha - Rudolf Steiner

"The author of the John Gospel indicates in various passages that what is communicated in the first chapters has to do with a certain kind and degree of initiation. You already know that there are different degrees of initiation. For example, in a certain form of oriental initiation, seven degrees can be distinguished and these seven degrees were designated by all sorts of symbolical names.

The first was the degree of the 'Raven,'

the second that of the 'Occultist,'

the third of the 'Warrior,'

the fourth that of the 'Lion.'

Amongst different peoples, who still felt a kind of blood relationship as the expression of their group-soul, the fifth degree was designated by the name of the folk itself

The sixth degree is that of the 'Sun-hero'

and the seventh that of the 'Father'."

Rudolf Steiner – "Gospel of John" – Chapter 5 - 'The Seven Degrees of Initiation'
https://wn.rsarchive.org/Lectures/GA100/English/LR1942/19071120p01.html

The Rosicrucian Method – 7 Steps

"While study schools the faculty of reason, and imaginative knowledge the life of feelings, knowledge of the occult script takes hold of the will. It is the path into the realm of creativity."

~ Rudolf Steiner

"1. Study…

2. Acquisition of imaginative knowledge…

3. Acquisition of the occult script…

4. Bringing rhythm into life, this is also described as preparing the philosopher's stone…

5. Knowledge of the microcosm, that is, of the human being's essential nature…

6. Becoming one with the macrocosm or great world…

7. Attaining godliness…"

Rudolf Steiner – "Stages of Rosicrucian Initiation" - Düsseldorf, December 15, 1907

7 steps - Esoteric Christianity – Rudolf Steiner

"1 – The Washing of the Feet - I am higher than the mineral, plant and animal, but to the lower kingdoms I owe my existence!...

2 – The Scourging – I must picture how it would be were all the suffering and sorrow possible in the world to come upon thee…

3 – The Crowning with Thorns - He must say to himself: —'Come what may, I must hold myself erect and defend what is holy to me.'…

4 – The Crucifixion - the pupil's body must become as foreign to his feelings as any external object…

5 – The Entombment - in an instant, a black curtain was drawn before the whole physical, visible world and as though everything had disappeared, as though the black curtain had been rent asunder and he looks into the spiritual world…

6 – The Resurrection - the pupil feels himself one with the entire earth-body…

7 – The Ascension - the complete absorption into the spiritual world…

Thus you see that the important thing in initiation is to influence the astral body in such a way by the indirect means of the day-experiences, that it may, when it is wholly free during the night, take on a new plastic form. When the human being in this manner, as an astral being, has given himself a plastic form, the astral body has become actually a new member of the human organism. He is then wholly permeated by Manas or Spirit-Self…"

Rudolf Steiner – "The Gospel of John" – Chapter 11 – 'Christian Initiation'

https://wn.rsarchive.org/Lectures/GA103/English/AP1962/19080530p01.html

Petalamund (Petal Mount)

Many of the teachings of Ageless Wisdom, which began before the written word, were passed down in oral traditions. Then as the written word progressed and man was more and more estranged from the spiritual world, and his own true spiritual nature, the written word had to become codified. The esoteric meaning had to become hidden within plain sight. A very big reason for this was due to the ongoing persecution of these traditions. Anything deemed heresy by dogmatic authority was always in danger of persecution.

To understand what was written down in plain view for all you had to be initiated into the esoteric meaning behind the words. In this way the tradition could still be handed down in a hidden way, yet as an 'open secret'.

Rudolf Steiner gave many lectures on the Gospels opening up the spiritual depth hidden in just this way. I would like here to give another example of how a story handed down through ages works in just this hidden spiritual way. The story is about the Holy Grail, it is the version written by Wolfram von Eschenbach, "Parzival".

The description of this coded language comes from Trevor Ravenscroft in "The Cup of Destiny".

Eschenbach begins with a description of the lands involved and where he found the story. He tells us that he found the tale in Anschau. Ravenscroft tells us that this is "not a physical location but a state of transcendent consciousness".

He tells us that outwardly the tale is of the adventures of knights, but inwardly, "it veils a prescribed path to the development of spiritual faculties for the attainment of higher levels of consciousness".

"The unique aspect of the western path, the quest for the Grail, is that it reverses the whole tradition of the eastern path to higher consciousness. For instance, all eastern traditions insist on the development of the *chakras* from below upwards... (now it is appropriate to develop these from above downward).

Foundational Flows

Wolfram von Eschenbach is describing a delicate subtle organ of perception. That is, a spiritual sense organ...In the Orient such organs are known as *'chakras'*, 'wheels' or 'lotus flowers'...

Where can we find in the artistic symbolism at the very beginning of the poem some hidden reference to such an evolution of consciousness from a dull, and almost dreamlike, state through period of acute intellectual doubt, to a total security of soul?...

The significant verses describe a city called Petalamund in some unspecified location in the Middle East. The city of the Petalamund is under siege and a battle is taking place in each of its 16 gates. And it is this city of Petalamund with the *sixteen* gates which, like a holographic, is nothing less than Wolfram's poem with its *sixteen* books seen as a whole. And so we find our first clue to the numerical structure of the work...

We must somehow find the key to break this medieval code and get behind the outer symbolism to discover the essential secret theme within this Grail poem. What this poet-initiate wishes to place in the very foreground of our minds is the path to the Grail itself and the faculties through which the Grail is unveiled. This path is apparently accomplished degree by degree ('Grail' is derived from 'gredalis' which means 'gradually') from dullness through doubt to security of soul, (saelde). The poet is telling us of the three stages in a radical evolution of consciousness through which humanity must pass in the quest for the Grail. Indeed, we watch Parzival, the hero of his tale, pass through such a personal development from naïve dullness, through the torment of doubt, to the final attainment of blessedness...

Our interpretation of the story has it structured into 16 adventures which relate to the development of a subtle organ of vision into the realities of the spirit. And we have shown how the original dull clairvoyance is reanimated of itself like the calyx of a flower opening out to unveil the blossom. It is the new 'eight-foldness' of this organ of vision which Buddha seeks to develop in man with his teaching of love and compassion on the path to a sublime consciousness which releases the human soul from the coils of karma…

It is the 16 petal lotus flower which Wolfram is describing through his symbolism of the city of Petalamund (Petal Mount). And it is this very organ which gives an insight into the working of the laws of destiny (karma). This particular organ, revealing the hidden rules of fate, is formed by sixteen distinct and different soul activities. Eight of these belong to a very ancient period in the evolution of human consciousness when man exercised them instinctively in a dull and darkened state of consciousness; while today it is possible to complete the development of the other eight qualities in a wakeful consciousness which is bright and clear. Indeed, Buddha himself describes them in his 'noble eightfold path'. And if these qualities are exercised then the eight activities that were developed earlier, and later atrophied, will again bear fruit of themselves."

- Trevor Ravenscroft – "The Cup of Destiny"

Here is a hint at the many interconnections to be found within this appendix -

Saturn – ♄ – Right Memory

Jupiter – ♃ – Right Opinion

Mars – ♂ – Right Word

Sun – ☉ – Right endeavor

Mercury – ☿ – Right Judgment

Venus – ♀ – Right Standpoint

Moon – ☽ – Right Deed

I Am – self-orientation- Right Examination

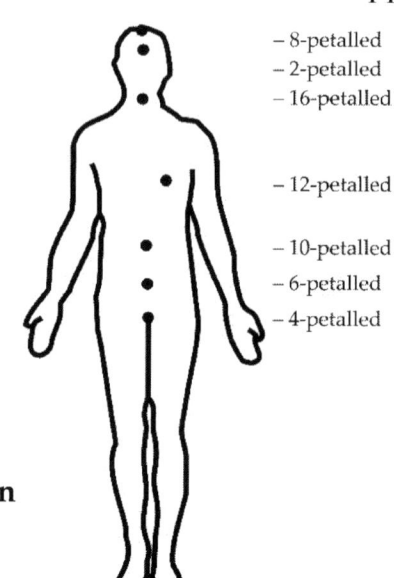

– 8-petalled
– 2-petalled
– 16-petalled
– 12-petalled
– 10-petalled
– 6-petalled
– 4-petalled

A comparison of the 8-fold path with Planets and Chakras (Lotus Flowers)

Appendix 2
Eurythmy

"And when illness of some kind or another overtakes the human being, then the forms corresponding to his divine archetype receive injury; here, in the physical world, they become different. What shall we do then? We must go back to those divine movements; we must help the sick human being to make those movements for himself. This will work upon him in such a way that the harm his bodily form may have received will be remedied.

Thus we look upon eurythmy as an art of harmonizing, just as in ancient clairvoyant times it was known that certain sounds, uttered with a special intonation, re-acted upon the health of man. But in those days one was shown how to affect the health by a more or less roundabout way, by means of the air, which worked back again into the etheric body. If one works more directly, if one makes the patient actually do the movements to the formation of his organs, - the point being, of course, that one knows what these movements really are, - (e.g., certain movements of the foot and leg correspond to certain formations right up into the head), - when one reproduces this, then there arises this aspect of curative eurythmy."

Rudolf Steiner – "Eurythmy as Visible Speech" – Dornach, June 24, 1924

Appendix 3
A brief list of the numbered meanings 1 – 26 Safety Energy Locks

1 – Prime mover, connecting extreme height with extreme depth

2 – Wisdom, life force for all creatures

3 – Understanding, the door defending against problems and discomforts

4 – The window

5 – Regeneration

6 – Balance, discrimination

7 – Victory, perfect life power

8 – Rhythm, strength, peace

9 – Ending of a cycle, beginning anew

10 – Out-pouring of limitless life power

11 – Justice, unloading of excess baggage

12 – Not my will but thy will

13 – Fertility, Love thine enemies

14 – Equilibrium, sustenance

15 – Joy and laughter

16 – Breaking down of existing forms for new ones, transformation

17 – Relaxation of mind and nerves

18 – Body consciousness

Foundational Flows

19 – Perfect balance, Authority and leadership

20 – Eternity. Everlasting

21 – Profound security, escape from mental bondage

22 – Complete, gathering and dispersal

23 – Proper circulation maintenance, controller of human destiny

24 – Understanding, harmonizing chaos

25 – Quietly regenerating

26 – Complete, that which was, is, and will be

Foundational Flows

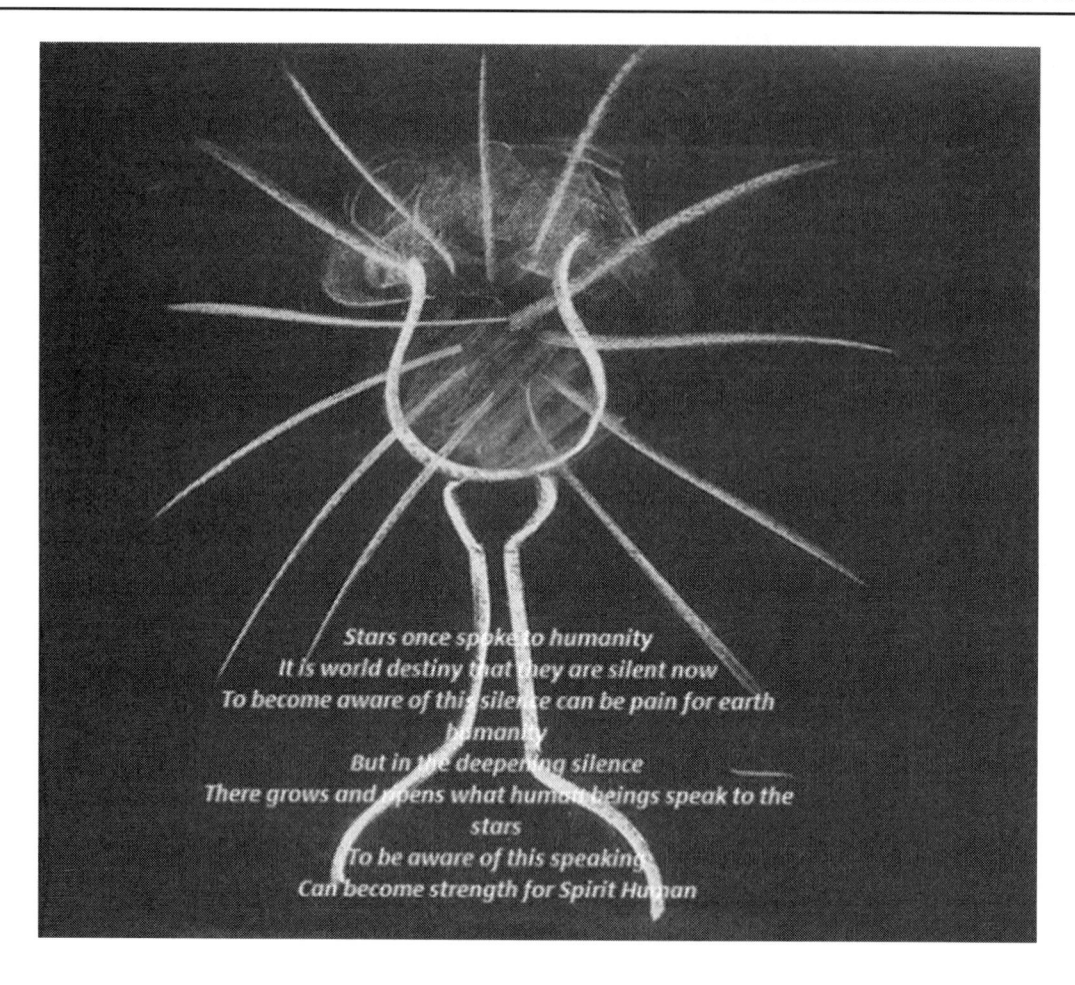

> Stars once spoke to humanity
> It is world destiny that they are silent now
> To become aware of this silence can be pain for earth humanity
> But in the deepening silence
> There grows and opens what human beings speak to the stars
> To be aware of this speaking
> Can become strength for Spirit Human

Above is a verse given by Rudolf Steiner. It is here superimposed onto a blackboard drawing he used in a lecture September 5, 1924.

About the Author

Stan Posey is a licensed Diplomat in Acupuncture and practices Chinese Medicine in Tucson, Arizona. Stan incorporates the use of Acupuncture, Chinese Herbal medicines, Tui Na Therapy and Manipulation, Craniosacral Therapy and Jin Shin Jyutsu in his practice. This combined strength of Stan's education and experience are the result of his strong interest in the sciences involved in alternative healing modalities.

Stan holds Bachelor of Science degrees in Bio-Agriculture and Botany from Arizona State University. He began his training in acupuncture and Traditional Chinese Medicine (TCM) at the California Acupuncture College and continued to build on that training at the Pacific College of Oriental Medicine, where he graduated in 1988.

A strong belief in the efficacy of a variety of healing methods led Stan to pursue additional training in Craniosacral Therapy through the Upledger Institute. He also has followed up with intensive training in Tui Na Therapy and Manipulation, with masters Vince Black OMD and Bill Helm. The other hands-on technique that Stan has been studying is Jin Shin Jyutsu, a Japanese Art brought to America by Mary Burmeister.

One of Stan's early interests was centered around what he has found to be the best self-learning tool - Evolutionary Astrology. He incorporates this method along with Rudolf Steiner's spiritual approach to astronomy and astrology - Astrosophy. This makes for a powerful and intensive adjunct in the treatment setting.

As an experienced and respected practitioner, Stan also shares his passion and knowledge of these healing arts through his teaching. Starting in 1996, Stan has taught at both the Arizona School of Acupuncture and Oriental Medicine and at the Asian Institute of Medical Studies. His dedication and passion to this field have had a positive and lasting impact on patients and students alike.

"Here's my description of my personal experience: During this series of sessions I directly experienced the re-ignition of my body's innate harmonizing force. The homework and recommended finger holds with breath support my connection to Spirit and help me maintain this. Looking back, it was the beginning of my return to my authentic self. I am forever grateful."

-- Angie E.

Made in the USA
Las Vegas, NV
09 March 2021